Shamanism, Ancestors and Transgenerational Therapy

BY THE SAME AUTHOR

We can integrate our hidden heritages instead of having them unconsciously driving our lives. We can also identify and rewrite the false or missing parts of our genealogy. With many illustrations the author shows how analyzing our ancestors' lives helps to understand problematic conditions and heals all kinds of symptoms. Goethe already explained: What we have received from our ancestors, we must assimilate until it becomes a part of ourselves if we want it to be an enrichment instead of a burden.

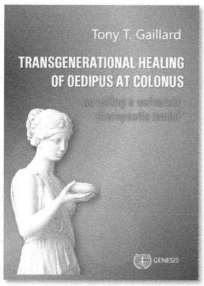

From the plague at the beginning of *Oedipus the King* to the glorious epilogue of *Oedipus at Colonus*, Sophocles' work is based on ancient unrecognized healing principles.

This book challenges some of our deep-seated contemporary prejudices. Instead of cutting our links with the environment that gave birth to us, as with the umbilical cord, by following Sophocles, we discover how to be better ourselves by symbolically integrating our roots. This way of restoring our belonging to the world frees us from the modern need to dominate it or instrumentalize it. More than ever, we need such a paradigm to deepen the meaning of our relationship to the world.

WWW.GENESIS-EDITIONS.COM

Shamanism, Ancestors and Transgenerational Therapy

Contemporary Practices

and Universal Wisdom

French original title:
« Chamanisme, rapport aux ancêtres et
Intégration transgénérationnelle »

Genesis Editions
18, rue De-Candolle, 1205 Geneva, Switzerland
www.genesis-editions.com
First Edition as "Shamanism, Ancestors and Transgenerational Integration", Ecodition, ISBN : 978-2-940540-19-8
2020 Second Edition Revised
ISBN 978-2-940540-40-2

Contents

Acknowledgments

My sincere thanks go to all those who made it possible to realize this new collective book, and first and foremost to the co-authors who gave this project its meaning and content. Their contributions illustrate that there is still room for projects which are innovative, multidisciplinary, and not necessarily politically correct - that is to say independent of any ideology. While some texts may have been intensely discussed before arriving at the published version, others are reproduced here strictly in their original forms, according to the wishes of their authors.

For their precious help, I also thank all those who participated in the transcription, translation or proofreading; Anne-Claude Barboni, Nicholas Brabhan, Laura Burkett, Dea Butcher, Lindi Dick, Michele Le Clech, William Metzgar, John Paval, Eva Morales, Jennifer Worthen.

Tony Thierry Gaillard, June 2020

Introduction

Tony T. Gaillard

Elders and traditional cultures emphasized active relationships between generations and with their ancestors. These exchanges connected the community with its roots and sources – both symbolic and mythological. When in harmony, these links would assure a balance for the collective as a whole as well as for each of its individual members. When these links were lost, shamans would be called upon to restore them and to heal the symptoms occasioned by this loss.

The healing potential and the importance of these links between generations and their ancestors have been rediscovered in numerous approaches in contemporary therapy: depth psychology, transgenerational psychoanalysis, family therapy, psychogenealogy, epigenetics, etc. Today we distinguish the conscious transmissions between generations, named "intergenerational", from the unconscious transmissions, named "transgenerational", which call for healing or therapy, that is to say "transgenerational integration".

As explained by the authors of this collection, the Ancients managed these links between generations and their ancestors in a variety of ways.

Ancestor cult, for example, kept the memory and transparency of family histories alive to prevent the consequences of unconscious legacies that could affect (or alienate) descendants. Martin Duffy explains: "In shamanic traditions it is important that the person is not just understood as an individual, they are connected to a network in their society as well as connected to their family lineage. Ancestral healing is very important in shamanism. And they are discovering this through science as well, in the field of epigenetics, where we can see that we inherit our physical characteristics, but we also can inherit much more. We can inherit memories of trauma, and generations later this can be manifesting in our current lives. One of the journeys we do in shamanism is to journey back and meet our ancestors to discover the power of our lineage. We often think of the defects we may have inherited, but it is really important to travel back to discover the power that we have from our ancestors too. In all shamanic cultures, working with the ancestors is vitally important because we are the ancestors of future generations to come[1]."

Ancestor cult pre-dates religions. It was widespread in Asia, Africa, and Europe, and was part of a desire for global harmony. When this harmony is not respected, the imbalance can be harmful to humans and to the rest of creation. Thus African totemism

---

[1] Martin Duffy (2015), "Ancient Wisdom, Modern Medicine", *Network Irland Magazin*, issue 93, Robinstown.

in spiritual tradition was not only concerned with men, but also with other creatures, including animals and plants.

No wonder that the ancestral customs have deified their ancestors, or have promoted some to the rank of intercessors with the gods, giving them some special functions: enhancing biological regeneration by their intervention in births and in actions to enhance soil fertility; ensuring the moral and social order; protecting their descendants whose peace, health, and well-being they assure and whom they warn by omen or oracle.

These traditional societies were aware of their origins and the life stories of their ancestors much more than we are today. Their collective memory particularly allowed recognizing the liabilities inherited from ancestors to avoid repeating the same mistakes, and to experience healing from them. The great writers constantly remind us of the importance of transgenerational, as Gustave Flaubert, "Many things would be brought to light if we knew our genealogy." When you start to clarify your family tree, its unsolved conflicts and the missing transmission form previous generations, you are already taking an active part to the process of integration. Without being aware of our transgenerational inheritance, profitable and/or distressing, our entire connection to our origins, to being and to life may be diminished.

Anyone could find and get in touch with their roots through their ancestors, showing many ways they care about them (anniversary ceremonies for example). The ancient wisdom says it is important to cultivate our rootedness and treat it when necessary - in the same way as we would care for a tree. Deepening these ties to ancestors is a way to reconnect with the healthy parts of our roots, to our mythological and spiritual origins.

In transgenerational integration work, what counts is to be proactive vis-à-vis our roots, to integrate them instead of passively undergoing our transgenerational inheritance. In order not to be possessed by this unconscious inheritance, Goethe said, "what you have inherited from your forefathers, acquire it to possess it." Giving life to one's ancestors within us becomes then a practice for oneself, a practice which, particularly in shamanism, extends to animals, plants, minerals, always with the aim to live in harmony with all creation. And finally, it is this love relationship in the world, including the ancestors, the heavens and the earth, animals, plants and all the life that animates the world, which is our relation to the "source". This is a kind of guarantor of a happy and prosperous life that all traditions have always taken to heart to protect.

As we will see in later chapters, these ideas are reflected in many ways in the ancient wisdom, in some rituals and especially in the first shamanic societies. They are also present in ancient sacred texts, including the Bible, Job (8.8) "Ask those of past generations, attend to the experience of their fathers. For we are of yesterday and we know nothing."

Gustav Glotz[2] explains that before the cult of individuality that we know today, the person (or the subject) was considered in relation to his family and not as individual. One blood was transmitted from generation to generation, forming a single being. In this perspective, a person who acted against the gods or against the laws of life, exposes his family and his descendants to pay the

---

2 Gustav Glotz, (1931), *Histoires grecques*, PUF, Genève.

moral and spiritual debt that he or she had contracted, even if he or she does not personally suffer the consequences,

The "cult" of individualization and repression (instead of psychological integration) that characterizes modern societies here shows its weaknesses. Too many secrets, non-integrated traumas, events and unfinished stories, are replayed between generations and disrupt the bonds of filiation. Due to an accumulation of alienating transgenerational inheritance, our society has lost the thread of the stories that bind generations together. Compared to the life of the ancients, it seems we have lost the feel for a living, spiritual parentage, rooting the sensation of being the architect of the creative updating of our heritage.

The recognition of transgenerational unconscious legacies comes right on time to apply not only therapeutic needs, but also to important cultural issues we are confronted with nowadays (increased infertility, disruption of natural forces, endemic epidemia, questions about parenting, Alzheimer's disease, etc.)

The articles in this collection share this perspective of re-appropriating, or updating, the old knowledge about transgenerational phenomena for the mutual enrichment of cultures, traditional and modern.

Pierre Ramaut will develop the relationship between the transgenerational psychoanalysis and shamanism, particularly around the issue of healing ghosts. "As transgenerational psychoanalysis, shamanism considers 'Ancestors disease' and their ghosts. These are dead 'not completely gone', who departed with an encrypted secret, in tragic circumstances, and still have a score to settle, or those who have not accepted the loss, or those whose body we never found, making it impossible for a mourning process to take place."

In an illuminating reading that combines anthropology, psychoanalysis and shamanism, Olivier Douville will return in his article to the question of ancestors and initiations.

Inspired by the ancestral methods, Elisabeth Horowitz will present ten therapeutic rituals to heal one's family tree. And to stay in the field of therapeutic applications, Myron Eshowsky addresses the issue of collective healing rituals for transgenerational trauma. As he explains: "The unhealed ancestral past stories exist in the spiritual space and are considered as factors causing disease and conflicts within the community. We pay past debts. If we have not cleared the slate, an invisible loyalty prompts us to repeat a moment of joy or unbearable sadness, injustice or a tragic death."

For her part, Iona Miller invites us through the doors and thresholds that separate us from the world of our ancestors. She will develop this theme, as well on the psychic, spiritual and material level, recalling the function of some monuments from the shaman and druidic culture, sculptures of aperture (vulvas) in the world of Mother Earth, the Sheela-Na-Ghi, for both initiation and protection.

In my article I will return to the source of the conflict that opposes the traditional culture and the modern since more than two millennia. To cope with the profound changes generated by the birth of our modern civilization (in Athens in the 5th century BC), Sophocles had to rewrite the old myth of Oedipus. He leaves us a model of healing the conflict between tradition and modernity that restores harmony between worlds. A model that gives pride to the integration of transgenerational inheritance as he said through the initiation of Oedipus to self-knowledge, knowledge of the gods and of the universe.

Finally, this collective book ends with an interview of C. Michael Smith on themes such as transmission, adaptation of ancient traditions to today's reality's world and to the way of the heart, honoring the earth, heaven and all the living.

Pierre Ramaut is a psychoanalyst who specialized in transgenerational psychoanalysis. After a long and classical psychoanalytic training (seminars of Lille and Brussels Clinical Section, "École de la Cause Freudienne" and "Champ Freudien"), Pierre Ramaut deepened his skills, in particular in transgenerational analysis. He is the founder of the SPRL Généasenss, a community whose aim is to enrich a set of information and tools in relation with transgenerational analysis. He has also imagined the "Commemoria" application to support life stories transmission. Moreover, Pierre Ramaut leads trekking in the desert and/or meetings with shamans in their native land.

Websites: www.geneasens.com, www.commemoria.com, www.waystobe.com and www.marcherpourprogresser.com

1

Transgenerational Psychoanalysis and Shamanism to Heal from Ghosts

Pierre Ramaut

With shamanism, we may think we are far outside the realm of rationality and over the limits imposed by a psychology which claims to be academic, neuroscientific, psychiatric and issued from classical psychoanalysis. Yet, oddly enough, far from academic preoccupations, transgenerational psychoanalysts and traditional shamans share at least one common therapeutic goal: to spot out and unveil ghostly figures, or phantoms, haunting the family lineage, so as to help their patients to become aware of and to verbalize the unthought-of unconsciously inherited. To heal a person, treating his family tree can make the difference, and transgenerational psychoanalysts know it, just as shamans do.

Currently, "classic psychology" does not have a model to account for the phenomena observed and described by various researchers on shamanism. Hence, practitioners who claim to align themselves with scientific theories, find themselves in a conceptual discomfort zone when trying to link these two fields that are transgenerational psychoanalysis and shamanism[1].

---

1 However, among the pioneers of depth psychology at the time (late 19th) there was a strong curiosity for parapsychology, telepathy, mediumship, with the first attempts of scientific experiments.

Thus it did require a lot of intelligence, openness, intellectual impertinence, boldness and courage (or foolishness some would say) to psychoanalyst Didier Dumas to bridge this gap and postulate that traditional shamanic practices could become an additional resource in the palette of therapeutic techniques of transgenerational analysis clinicians.

Psychogenealogy or transgenerational psychoanalysis?

The word "psychogenealogy" currently covers so many different practices (ranging from the most serious to the most eccentric) that, for my part, I prefer using the terms "transgenerational psychoanalysis" that we owe to Didier Dumas. It has the advantage of accurately locating the field in which this discipline is exercised, namely the scope of the unconscious.

It is also important to note, since the confusion exists in the general public and often in the media, that transgenerational transmission is an unconscious transmission between generations, whereas intergenerational transmission is a conscious transmission between generations.

Like many traditional cultures, transgenerational psychoanalysis draws attention to the potential influence of traumas, unsaid secrets, unfinished tasks and undone mourning left by ancestors, which are thereby unconsciously transmitted to the subsequent generations. It also reminds us that the familial unconscious interferes with the individual unconscious.

Transgenerational psychoanalysis is rooted as much in the field of psychology being called scientific and rational, as in the fields of art, mythology, intuition and the teachings of some spiritual traditions including shamanism.

When dealing with these new fields of psychology, one need to accurately define several concepts to try to explain, articulate and highlight the possible complementarities that connect transgenerational psychoanalysis and shamanism.

Some concepts in transgenerational psychoanalysis

In transgenerational psychoanalysis, the unconscious is not only determined by the events of our childhood, but also by what is transmitted from generation to generation, following its own rules. We are born already "loaded" of legacy content that comes to us from far away and that are called "ghosts" or "phantoms".

The crypt and the ghost

Two psychoanalysts, Nicholas Abraham and Maria Torok, have provided a first definition of the word "ghost", to define a particular content of the unconscious. It has never been conscious and was passed on generations from the unconscious of a parent to the unconscious of a child.

The origin of a ghost lies in an event remained secret, unsaid, unconfessed, canned in a psychic crypt, which then comes back to haunt a descendant through different symptoms, spoken words (like a ventriloquist) and bizarre acts.

Ghost as left unthought-of entity in the genealogy

A child growing up amidst unsaid things is paradoxically confronted with words, reactions and attitudes of adults, the meaning of which he cannot understand, but which make him feel that something important is hidden from him and censored. This situation creates paradoxical injunction that will generate failures (holes and lack of symbolism) in his psychic construction.

For psychiatrist and psychoanalyst Serge Tisseron[2], the traumas that were experiences by a first generation, but were hidden or repressed (not psychologically integrated), can ricochet on the next generations. The state of the first event that had remained secret and which is encrypted in the psyche will evolve over its transmission across generations. The secret which was unsayable for its first carrier becomes unnamable for the second generation and, even worse, unthinkable for the third generation.

In the same vein, psychoanalyst Didier Dumas[3] speaks about the ghost as a "lack to speak," generally generated from a traumatic family event that involved sex (rape, incest, illegitimate children ....) death (suicide, crime, violent death unmourn...), since these two themes almost always fit in an "emptiness of language". Collective trauma, such as war, deportations, etc. can become a "family unthought-of" as well, that is passed down on to the subsequent generations, waiting to be healed.

This family unthought-of works surreptitiously, quietly and stealthily in the unconscious, forming psychic unspeakable objects which have the power to be transmitted from unconscious to unconscious in the lineage until a descendant resumes and bears the "transgenerational mandate."

---

2 Tisseron, S. (2011), *Les secrets de famille*, PUF, Paris, et (1995), *Le psychisme à l'épreuve des générations*, clinique du fantôme, Dunod, Paris.

[3] Didier Dumas (1989), *Hantise et clinique de l'autre*, Aubier, Paris, et, *La Bible et ses fantômes*, Desclée de Brouwer (2001), Paris.

The transgenerational mandate

Indeed, Ancient Chinese people considered that a "transgenerational mandate" arising from affiliation to the ancestors could be bestowed by heaven upon one of the ultimate descendants of the lineage. The latter is then "mandated" to take over the unfinished stories of the genealogical tree and forced to integrate that genealogical and familial unthought-of in his lifetime.

As Taoism has not rejected it shamanic roots, unlike other religions, Taoists believe there are links between ancestry and its effects on an individual's life

If we are born with a life project that is no doubt personal, it is also related to our heritage. A transgenerational mandate works in us, and puts us on the path of who we are.

In this view, working on the family tree allows the heir to starts integrating, here and now, his multiples mandates, to feel what can put him in true resonance with himself and encourages him to find its point of insertion and action in the world to accomplish what Carl Gustave Jung called "the process of individuation.[4]"

Becoming aware of the ghost and being able to name it

The carrier of a generational ghost is haunted by a psychic legacy content, an event that another has lived in an earlier generation. He can't say absolutely nothing about it because of a lack of speech and lack of conscious intergenerational transmission of the inaugural event.

---

4 Carl Gustav Jung (1990), *L'Âme et le soi, renaissance et individuation*, Albin Michel, Paris.

One of the major goals of the patient as part of a transgenerational analysis will thus be to become able to name his ghost or ghosts (phantoms), that is to say, to symbolize them in order to integrate this psychic legacy into his personal history.

The transgenerational analysis invites the practitioner to adopt an attitude in which he assumes to seek, with and for his client, which way to go to find the missing information. This attitude is exactly the one adopted by traditional shamans with their patients!

The genosociogram

The genosociogram is one of the tools of transgenerational psychoanalysis. It is a kind of "fantastical" family tree completed by the major life events and by their emotional context that allows the patient to become aware of the ties that unite and bind him to his ancestors, his collaterals, their roles and that can also highlight the repetition of phenomena : accidents, illnesses, unresolved grief, unsaid events, birthday syndromes (or repetition syndromes), family myths, etc.

In a single glance, the genosociogram allows one to connect and articulate a large and complex amount of information, a performance that the left brain (analytical, sequential) is unable to perform alone. Thanks to the right brain, the genosociogram allows users to capture and become aware a full set of meaningful relationships, pictorially, globally and instantaneously.

Pre-verbal structures of the mind

Psychoanalysis usually explores and analyzes the deepest dimension and most unconscious dimensions of the psyche through dream since pre-verbal structures of the mind consist mainly of images and sensations.

These preverbal structures of the mind known as "original", or "primal", manifest themselves in the dream world of patients and other psychic manifestations like trance. And it is in this original construction of the human mind that shamanic journeys occur.

From the fetal stage until the third year, and before the acquisition of speech, the primal mental activity is the only one at work in the child's psyche and it is thanks to this primal psychic activity that the child unconsciously duplicates his parents' system of representation and that he begins to speak their language without having to learn it.

For psychoanalyst Didier Dumas, the psychological construction of the human being is not individual, as Freud postulated, but transgenerational, meaning that it is determined, at its core, in the children of less than three years, by the duplication of the unconscious mental structures of his parents. As these were built by duplicating the mental structures of grandparents, this explains why ancestral problems that transgenerational psychoanalysis calls ghosts (or phantoms) can be transmitted over generations.

During this special time, before the age of three, the baby lives in a communal psyche which is that of his host family, in which the primal mental activity allows him to be at once himself and those who support him, duplicating their mental structures. This primal mental activity explains why schizophrenics can confuse their own body with that of another, or why the paranoiac people attribute their own thoughts to another person.

This mental activity does not completely disappear by growing up, it continues to work through adulthood. It manifests itself through number of psychic experiences with images and sensations like in dreams, mediumship, telepathy, clairvoyance, hypnosis, trance or shamanic journey.

This is also why most psychotic and autistic children often have unusual faculties studied in parapsychology, such as, for example, clairvoyance, and precognition, the ability to numb oneself or to leave one's body and other gifts similar to those of great mystics or shamans.

The originality of transgenerational psychoanalysis is to take a deep interest in this primal mental activity and to award an unusual place to images and sensations.

Concepts in Shamanism

Traditional shamanic practices meet those of transgenerational psychoanalysis insofar as "trance" and "shamanic journeys" are immersed in these primal strata of the mind which are made up with the universe of sensations and mental images.

In his book *Shamanism, An Expanded View of Reality,*[5] Shirley Nicholson and her colleagues explain that shamanism has at its disposal a vast and ancient knowledge that offers the possibility to work on mental planes so far neglected by psychoanalysis, such as for example, communication from unconscious to unconscious, collective dimensions, cultural and social mental structures, cultural relationship to death and questions about the survival of the spirit.

---

5 Shirley Nicholson et coll. (1990), *Shamanism - An Expanded View Of Reality,* The Theosophical publisher, London.

The sickness and the healing of Ancestors

As transgenerational psychoanalysis, shamanism takes into account "the Ancestor's syndrome" and their ghosts. These are deceased ancestors "not completely gone", who left with an encrypted secret, in tragic circumstances, still having stories to finish, or those whose losses have never been accepted, or those whose bodies have never been found, making it impossible for the mourning work to be achieved.

Shamans are men and women who voluntarily change their state of consciousness, to communicate in another time and space dimension with the various forces of nature and of the universe, which allows them to heal the members of their tribe and improve the cohesion and the condition of their social group. These unusual experiences enable them to reach for therapeutic information (remember that the ability to search for information on a "family unthought-of" is key to understanding the relationship between shamanism and transgenerational psychoanalysis).

One of the most common mistakes that is made about shamanism is to consider it as a kind of rare and exotic human behavior, even a dangerous one: an archaic anomaly, a vestige of the secret origins of our sacred life. But shamanism shares basic characteristics with the immemorial traditions that mark history, which have appeared in all the established societies, including the Western society. In every culture we find myths that account for encounters between humans and singular entities, called spirits, God, deities, angels, demons, apparitions as well as phantoms....

By definition, a shaman is someone who works and collaborates with "spirits", in altered states of consciousness, in order to accumulate inner powers, to find for his patient or community, these inaccessible pieces of information (the familial unthought-of) and solutions for therapeutic and/or social issues.

The Reality of Spirits?

For Richard Noll, "Minds are like transpersonal forces in motion that we experience in us or through us, but which are not animated by us alone."

Shamans are related to a realm where spirits provide help and wisdom, but are these spirits mere projections of the unconscious of the shaman, or on the contrary, do they have an objective reality?

All cultures have described spirits as transpersonal forces that animate or go through the shaman, but as being almost always out of our control. As Carl Gustav Jung said: "There are things in the psyche which I do not produce, but which produce themselves and have their own life."

These forces, mostly personified (power animals, dead ancestors, etc.), are autonomous entities with their own independence. In the ordinary conscious state, the shaman usually cannot contact them or make them work, but in the state of shamanic consciousness (ECC), he can contact them and sees them clearly.

Shamans do not see these phenomena as a product of their mind, in the sense that they would be seen as a projection of their own mind. Their brain is used to access a door from where one enters into another independent existing reality. The shamanic universe goes beyond the simple "content" of the human brain. For many shamans, the crucial part of initiation is to get in touch with the right spirit, that is to say, with those who will become the guardian spirits.

Psychoanalyst Carl Gustav Jung had a guardian spirit that he called Philemon. It appeared to him as a bearded old man or as a prophet who gave him essential advice. Philemon was both the initiator of Jung, he who delivered teachings, the protector indicating the right track, and sometimes one that was purposefully misleading.

Protecting Spirits, power animals and lost ancestors

The transmission of cultural traditions and of some practical advice by shaman masters is an indispensable aspect of initiation. However, almost universally it is accepted that the novice receives his knowledge from spirits and that the greatest lessons are taught by spiritual guides. The novice uses the powers of the guardian spirit (whether it takes a human or an animal form) that he met in his initiatory visions. This spirit introduces him to protector spirits to whom he asks for help in healing and divination sessions (information search including transgenerational ghosts). These protecting spirits are deemed essential; without them, the shaman can do nothing.

The structure of the shamanic universe: the three worlds.

In shamanic cultures, the universe would consist of three cosmic levels (heaven, earth and the underworld) often called "the world of the top", "the middle world", "the world below", connected by a central axis through which the shaman can communicate with each of these regions.

Carl Gustav Jung compared the human mind to a vast story house, each of which contained several potential. He showed that most people in the modern era only live on one or two floors, forgetting the other. "With this wonderful house, on several floors, that we call the human mind, it seems that we should turn to shamans to help us before it is too late, to recover what we have lost in regard to the human soul."

In shamanic learning, rituals, trials, ingestion of psychoactive substances, prayer, meditation, fasting and guidance of teachers in this world and in the other, all the floors of the mind are explored. What may seem crazy for someone from the outside is for the shaman a mere stroll into the multidimensional mind, including the original structures in which transgenerational ghosts duplicate from generations to generations.

The shaman is a specialist of ritual communication

The shaman is primarily a person of connection, a mediator, a bridge between the forces and the elements of the three worlds of the universe.

The state of shamanic consciousness corresponds to the mystic state where one comes into harmony with the "grand unified order of things"; and the shaman "is moving in the structure of the universe" and communicates with the entire nature, including the animals, the spirits, including those of the "dead not properly deceased" which transgenerational psychoanalysis calls ghost. This gives to the shaman the ability to restore harmony thanks to his symbolic action between ordinary and non-ordinary dimensions of reality.

The ordinary state of consciousness would just be an illusion

For some shamans, our ordinary state of consciousness is merely an illusion, a "lie" and any significant event in our world would just be the result of events hidden in the other dimension. In this sense, the role of the shaman is to intervene in this other dimension to obtain an effect on our illusory dimension, called the "consensual reality".

The Shaman's states of consciousness

The shaman has the ability to orchestrate his different states of consciousness, those which allow him to bridge the gap between ordinary reality and transpersonal levels. However, we should distinguish these altered states of consciousness (induced by the drum, the singing, the fasting, the thermal control, the sensory deprivation or the use of psychedelic substances) called state of shamanic consciousness (SSC), from the pathological altered states of consciousness studied in psychology.

When the shaman operates a healing in the shamanic conscious state, he uses mental resources that are not accessible to the men of the modern world anymore, or which they are not interested in because of their dependence towards the logical and rational conscious thoughts.

Dreaming is also an integral part of shamanism. Shamans call the spirits in dreams and also receive their power and the necessary information for the healing of their "patients" through this channel.

Protector spirit and spiritual guides

The protector spirit, met in these initiatory visions, often takes the form of a "power animal" and the novice calls for it (whether it takes a human or an animal form) to be protected as he enters into altered states of consciousness that are potentially dangerous (shamanic state of consciousness "SSC") and when he travels in trance in the upper and lower worlds.

This spirit also introduces the shaman to other guardian spirits to whom he may ask for help during healing and divination sessions. These guardian spirits are essential to the work of the shaman; without them, the shaman cannot engage anything. Sometimes these spiritual guides are ancestors.

The path of becoming a shaman is tortuous and more than one who is called procrastinates before undertaking this disturbing mandate. This is because the shamanic path requires both to engage in the disintegration and total dissolution of one's being, to penetrate chaos in a conscious way, but also to accept social isolation, the suffering that come with extraneous thoughts and substantial risks of personality alteration that can be assimilated to madness by the uninitiated observer.

To Honor the Dead, Well or Badly Deceased

In this link that interests us between shamanism and transgenerational analysis, it is important to note that the focus of transgenerational psychoanalysis goes to these "improperly deceased ancestors" who have become "ghosts". To be more exact, we should say "the Dead that un-properly died", and who therefore could not access the status of favorable ancestors for offspring, because, as Olivier Douville writes it very well: "Death does not in itself alone transform the deceased into an ancestor. This transformation depends on a ritualized passage that registered the deceased, gradually, in the world of the dead."

Psychotics or Shamans?

The shaman has often been called the "wounded healer", the "crazy half cured," the "badly integrated individual." It is true that many of them have been through a terrible psychological crisis before their vocation. The shamanic initiatory experience is very similar (if not identical) to certain states of mental illnesses such as schizophrenia. However, it is quite clear that the shaman was not only physically or mentally wounded, but that he has also been cured in one way or another; he (or she) is actually a "cured healer."

This healing sometimes occurs spontaneously, as is the case for some schizophrenics who have apparently gone through a true shamanic initiatory crisis with the support of phenomena from the "inner and higher worlds" and which they get out of, after a recovery period. Most often, however, in tribal societies, the future shaman is assisted in its initiatory crisis by a whole tradition of shamanic methods of teachings and masters who train the neophyte. This tradition represents the legacy of those who have gone the same path, who have to some extent drawn its graphic and have learned to deal with the phenomena that may take place there. The shaman is also the one who explores by himself the fields of disease, decay, mental suffering and death. He (or she) is deeply familiar with human distress and the possibility of transcending agony. Thus, the personal experience of the shaman in the realm of suffering is the starting point for his compassionate action in society.

The shaman calls the spirits in an altered state of consciousness that he deliberately induced, a state that occupies only a limited part of his time since he also needs to continue to fulfill his social role. On the contrary, a patient is the victim of the voices he hears, who mock him and generally criticize him mercilessly. Sometimes they even can drive him to suicide. A person with hallucinations and visions, who is torn and driven without control in the depths, can easily be accused of being schizophrenic, while a shaman has the ability to control himself and can connect with his hallucinations without feeling his mind rip. One might expect that the shaman in trance might completely lose the control of his faculties of perception and be overwhelmed by fear. But it is precisely his ability to gain "wisdom from madness" that distinguishes him from the schizophrenic. Thus the journey of the shaman is dependent on his will.

A cultural question

How is it that some people come successfully to an end of these crises and others not? Why do some people develop paranoid and psychotic behavior? One of the possible factors is the socio-cultural acceptance of the experience of the crisis. The spirit world, the dreams and visions of the shaman may seem abnormal according to our cultural criteria whereas in shamanic cultures, they are all part of the reality and of the common belief in a world full of spirits which are capable of investing individuals and cause disease.

Thus, the cultural environment can be either a hindrance or a support to the reformulation of the shamanic journey depending on the way it will judge that experience as undesirable and negative - thus evoking shame, anxiety and alienation feelings - or positive and welcoming - opening a culturally accepted way to the experience. In other words the same experience in a culture like ours produces psychotic. While in a shamanic culture, it will produce a shaman. There may be many shamans who haunt the halls of our asylums, confined there, and which in other circumstances and with a different initiation, could have become resources for others and for society instead becoming poor mangled souls.

Shamans and psychoanalysts, an analogy?

There is an obvious parallel between the shamanic initiatory experience and the experience - also initiatory - of a psychoanalytic cure. Isn't a psychoanalyst also someone who has lived a "downward spiral" that led him to call to another (psychoanalyst) for help and that, at the end of his psychoanalytic treatment, transformed by the analytic experience, decides to turn to occupy the place of the analyst and to start listening to his fellows?

Until it has not been absorbed, the traumatic past of our ancestors continues to project itself unconsciously and parasitize our image of the world, to influence more or less seriously our relationship with reality. The more the mind will actively repress certain events, the more it will resist to any possibility of change the way it looks at them, and be able to break free from prejudice (be it familial or personal), which leads us naturally to the question of the timelessness of the psyche.

Freud believed that the soul of the dreamer went through another temporality then the one of the sleeper, to report from his "inner world", namely the unconscious, some awareness. The Freudian dreaming journey that distinguishes the time of the dreamer from that of the sleeper seems analogue to the travel of the shaman in search for information and solutions for his patient in another space-time reality. The integration of past traumas is therefore closely linked to the question of temporality. Even after several generations, the heirs to the sufferings of their ancestors still remain fixed to that time when these sufferings occurred. The impact of a trauma therefore does not belong to a linear space-time, and as long as we have to deal with "a past that has not passed away", the descendants remain captive within time of the effects of unsaid, unnamed and non-integrated traumas. What has

31

not been assimilated is always present, whether consciously or not. Integration gaps have no temporal limit, and time does not really act on what is repressed in the unconscious, it continues and is passed on from generation to generation. The action of the ancestral trauma will therefore extend over generations by hampering the growth and natural development of the offspring, which will remain frozen at the time of the traumatized ancestor as long as it is not metabolized, here and now.

Transgenerational psychoanalysts and Shamans: A same quest for vision, but with different tools

Transgenerational psychoanalysts and shamans are engaged on a similar path to help patients to appropriate unknown unconscious psychic parts. Both operate in a multiple temporality in search of a "vision" and of new information about the unfinished and unthought-of of the family tree of their patients, but each with its own tools.

The transgenerational psychoanalyst brings the individual to hunt for family secrets, to complete his genealogy, and to reset his family history in various contexts to help his client to identify his or her "crypts", and to name his (or her) "ghost (s)" with the help of the genosociogram.

The shamanic method is identical in all shamanic societies: It is about entering the patient, becoming the patient, and then restoring a sense of interrelatedness. The work of the shaman is fulfilled in the realm of the imagination, he operates a visualization which then becomes an instrument for the healing through the experience of an ultimate reality that he will restructure to produce a transformation in his patient.

In an altered state of consciousness (shamanic state of consciousness SSC), the shaman uses transpersonal healing images, which implies that the information is accessible from the consciousness of a person to that of another. This transpersonal imagery has a direct therapeutic effect on patients throughout the vivid images it engenders and this requires the existence of information channels that can be located in the original and preverbal strata of our mental construction as Didier Dumas theorized it.

Conclusion

Psychoanalysis has shown that symptomatic manifestations disappear when the original conflict, usually unconscious, is reintegrated. Applied to transgenerational phenomena, the same conception matches the symptoms of ancestral memories that have been split out, denied or repressed, to protect from the monstrous and unspeakable/unsayable related event. Alienation is therefore demanding that a verb, related to these unassimilated experiences from previous generations, be restored. The simple layout in words can undo the negative consequences of transgenerational inheritance. For the transgenerational psychoanalyst as for the shaman, the therapeutic processes convene unconscious entities that participate in the process of integration and transformation of symptoms into symbols.

Olivier Douville Ph.D. is a clinician psychologist, psychoanalyst and anthropologist, international speaker, member of the French Association of Anthropologist and of the Association of the encounter Anthropology /Psychoanalysis on Socialization Processes

Lecturer in clinical psychology at the University of Paris 10-Nanterre and at the University of Paris 7 Denis-Diderot, member of the Research Center of Psychoanalysis, Medicine and Society at the University of Paris 7, he is the author and co-author of numerous books and articles.

His website :

https://sites.google.com/site/olivierdouvilleofficiel/

2

Splitting off from the Dead, Establishing the Ancestor

Olivier Douville

In this article[1] I will analyze a few points of interest in anthropology that are likely to inspire research in the "transgenerational" field. They are related on the one hand to the links to the ancestors, and, secondly, to this function assigned to the shamans of separating the worlds, those of the dead from those of the living. These traditional practices, ancient and still continuing today, offer anthropological references to numerous developments that abound nowadays in the "transgenerational" area.

I will begin by briefly recalling the importance given to the ancestors in traditional societies before addressing the theme of initiation. The reader will then better understand the task of the shaman, obstetrician of the world, who guarantees a balance between the different worlds and is in charge of restoring relationships with ancestors to benefit from their benevolence. This

---

1 This article sums up two conferences entitled: « Ancestors and Transmission » at a colloquium in Chengdu (China), April 2014, and « The Craziness of The Shaman, a Controversy », Meetings at Ville-Evrard (France), June 2014.

function does not fail to evoke the work on the family tree of some contemporary therapists. The issue of un-alienating the subject, central to the work of transgenerational integration[2], finds an instructive parallel in shamanic cultures.

The symbolic and imaginary relations to our ancestors generally relate to missing persons and how they departed (honored or not, died well or in unclarified circumstances). In this regard the theme of the ancestor refers to a kind of "depth for life" that circulates between the living and the dead. On this point anthropologists join the considerations of therapists.

The Ancestor and the child

Death does not by itself turn a deceased into an ancestor. This transformation depends on a ritualized passage that registered the deceased, gradually, in the world of the dead. In some societies, anthropologists, like Robert Hertz, are talking about a double funeral. The first funeral is devoted to the treatment of the corpse; during this period, the spirit of the dead, because of its ambivalent nature, can be dangerous. The second heals both the appetite of the spirit of the dead for destruction and his manic wish to disrupt the ordinary course of existence of the living.

These double funerals can thus transform the dead into an ancestor, who then become beings with name who can be addressed in a ritualized way for celebrating the lineage and filiations. This

---

2 Tony T. Gaillard (2020), *Transgenerational Integration: Healing the Inherited Burden*, Genesis Editions, Geneva.

world of ancestors is classically composed of two fractions: the direct ancestors who are often in a close genealogical link (fourth, fifth or sixth generation before the living adult who refers to them) and mythical ancestors, who are transcendental figures localized at the junction of myth and history, or assimilated to the totemic entities which Freud attempted to identify in the functioning of the unconscious.

Societies with archives and "ancestral altars" (i.e., ritual seats in West Africa, ancestral altars in China and Viet Nam) can harbor archival documents that stack shelves or engraved lines covering a very large number of generations (sometimes up to twenty-five).

In a traditional world, still living in balance, it is often observed that the debts to the ancestors are divided differently between the living people according to the degree of ancestry they are dealing with. While distant ancestors are the guarantors of the standards and ideals, it is in the name of the closest ancestors that arrangements are made around the small debts and discussions about the transmissions of goods and privileges. In short, we honor the first and negotiate with the latter. The language with the distant ancestors, these ultimate authority figures, is much codified, especially around the very ritualistic sacrifices. In contrast, the discussion is more open between the living, to determine what is due to close ancestors and how one can reconcile with them to obtain their benevolence. In his analysis of his definition of the man as a "Being in debt", Marcel Mauss says that there are always moments of imbalance in the combinatorial of alliances and debts.

The theme of the ancestor is interesting because it allows us to situate what is at work when these links to ancestry are damaged or lost. Gaps that are today appearing in transgenerational analysis, for example around the family secrets and other difficult transmission in the lineage, are important sources of alienation.

In anthropology, the issue of child-ancestor is representative of this issue in the lineage. Its healing calls for a symbolic filiation to be restored, guaranteeing a differentiation of the persons. What is it about? The child must be shaped by a ritual, and if necessary, cured of this disease that these so-called traditional African societies fear. This disease that affects some children would be due to a condensation between the child's body and the mind of the ancestor. If it was not treated, transgenerational analysis would here recognize a classic alienation process, that of a "parentalization" of the child. It is important thus to properly define the relationship to the child just born, from the relationship to the world of the ancestors. Purgation, for example, will be made through the burial of the placenta, something that African families still much demand in their maternity facilities.

Answers may vary to the question asked by the external observer, "Why do you bury the placenta?" Some will tell you that the burial of the placenta is important because, "It's not good, this piece of flesh is dirty, so we must bury it". Yet these hygienic spirits do not spend their time burying all that is not good and everything that is dirty. This is rather a short explanation anyway. Others will tell you that you must bury the placenta because the placenta is a double of the child[3].

---

3 The first conquerors of Cambodia told, for example, that when they were received by the local chiefs, they saw right next to the throne an

This burial ritual of the placenta is an example of what anthropologists can bring to contemporary therapeutic practices concerning the strategy of transgenerational un-alienation, allowing the child to exist as himself.

In continuation of these issues about differentiating what belongs to the world of the ancestors and what refers to the mortal human, the shaman's work is particularly relevant here. Work that contributes to the good balance of people and communities should be able to inspire the contemporary field addressing "transgenerational" issues. Highly significant, related aspects of shamanic practices deserve some development.

The shaman at the border of worlds

Shamanism is a practice reserved for those who can be healers but are not always, since it is not always necessary. Their main function is to mediate between humans and nature spirits or sometimes with missing people. Originally shamans, whose practice has been known by Westerners since the eighteenth century, belonged to a group of people in northern Siberia, named the "Tungus". They give the name "shaman" to their religious "experts", who includes priests, sorcerers, magicians and soothsayers. This election can be seen as a curse, something the future shaman cannot refuse and that he accepts after a series of typical crises that are decisive initiations: inability to absorb food, long wild wanderings, trance, twilight experiences. From Siberia, shamanic practices have spread along the lines of migration and have crossed the Bering Strait and extended into Australia.

---

overloaded chair with ornaments and precious stones on which a painted coconut containing the monarch's placenta was placed.

The starting points of anthropological research are the relations between the shaman and the spirits and between the shaman and the community of the living people. These researches bring us into an encounter with an amazing character. With no fixed identification, or decisive gender identification, whether the shaman is like a dead person or living ghost or a living person is not always clear. The shaman can certainly stand as being the one by which the dead are returning. There can therefore be some identity confusion, in any case from the perspective of a Westerner conditioned by his modern culture.

The work of Saladin d'Anglure[4] shows this complexity, like those of Jung and Mircea Eliade. The first psychoanalysts who went into indigenous land, Rivers[5] and Roheim[6], were particularly passionate about the topic of the ecstatic dreams in shamanism. Studies multiplying, the term of shaman is then extended, first to Canada's Native healers especially in the area of Quebec, the Algonquin (Jacques Leroux), to the Iroquois and to the medicine man, descending the American continent down to South America.

---

4 Bernard Saladin d'Anglure, anthropologist (Ph'D of Ethnology at the University of Montreal, and in the "École pratique des hautes études de Paris"). He has done several researches in Canada and has been the assistant of the famous anthropologist Claude Lévi-Strauss.
5 Williams Halse Rivers, psychoanalyst and anthropologist was one of the very first ethnologists to study Freud's works.
6 Géza Róheim is an American ethnologist and psychoanalyst from Hungary, born in Budapest in 1891 and who died in 1953 in New York. After a long classical training, he studied anthropology in Leipzig and Berlin with a philosophical Ph'D. He studied the inaugurate works of the pioneers in psychoanalysis, Freud, Sandor Ferenczi, Karl Abraham, Otto Rank.

The dream, a royal initiator path?

A common point between different shamanic traditions turns specifically around the issue of dreams and shamanic journey. Moreover, there is no doubt unfair to talk about shamanism for peoples or cultures that do not give the dream a leading role in the initiation of adolescents.

Thanks to my friend Jacques Leroux, I lived a while in the Algonquin land. In his company, I talked to some of the Elders, the old people of this village who do not have our harsh, selfish, meticulous sense of property; houses and goods are quite easily passed on. As Maurice Godelier[7] rightly pointed out, one cannot understand anything of the general system of exchange or gift, if we ignore the object that cannot be shared, which cannot be given. This invaluable object, not exchangeable and non-negotiable, having no exchange value, or even a using value, is like a vanishing point of organization for all exchanges or negotiations. Negotiations are done in the shade of the tree, under the protection of which nothing can be negotiated.

This object, I was told by my Algonquin friend, is a gamebag. What is this gamebag? It is the object that is given in the initiation. To understand its importance, we must understand what kind of initiation we are talking about. At the end of childhood, the youth goes through a necessary isolation to get him out of

---

7 He was Claude Lévi-Strauss' assistant when teaching at the "Collège de France". In 1975, he was elected director of the High School for Social Sciences, and in 1995, he creates in Marseille the CREDO (Research and Documentation Center on Oceania).

fusion with his first partners and also away from all that would be a morbid tendency for solitude or self-foundation.

The initiation[8] is a solitary experience, together with many other people. Initiation associates the collective with the singular. The young will thus be isolated in the forest. No one brings him any food; he has to manage on his own, but he is still recommended to fast as much as possible. Then, the day he makes an important dream, he will be initiated by his peers (so he does not undergo these harsh trials that have hit the headlines in Africa and South America). In his dream, suddenly, intermediary beings come to him who take him to a world that is neither heaven nor earth. In this rapture (where anguish still gives its alarm calls), a world opens to him. A world that carries him, moves him and, again, shapes him.

This youth, older than the world, more tender than any sapling is presented to the sun, to the moon, to the stars, to the important animals, eagle and salmon. And what is said in the Algonquin wisdom, both remembering and inventing its myths on the magical screen of ceremonials, is that once he has had that dream, the child informs the chiefs of the village who will come to him, with the village elders and parents too. They ask him if he has had a good dream so that the way is free for the youth to tell his dream. But he is also asked to write the name he received in a secret language and, initiated to the powers of the script, the youth who now possesses a secret, writes on the inside skin of his game bag the name he received.

---

8 Initiation is not reserved only to boys, as evidenced by the Africanist literature, whether by Robert Jaulin in "The Death of Sara" or by Griaule in "Dogon Masks."

42

At the end of the initiation, the youth becomes an adult. No one can claim the right to see what is inside the bag. Aristotle has his own explanation of initiation: "At the end of initiation, we will not know more, but something has happened by which we will be done differently."

One thing that was confirmed to me by my anthropologist friend is that the Algonquins have given themselves a solid theory of the dream life, which rests on the distinction between two types of dream. There is the typical dream of initiation that ends with the inscription. But another type of dream can manifest during this extraordinary journey, within this rapture from cosmic elements and archetypal animals. As for the first kind of dream, the elements which the youth is presented appear fixed and dumb, in the second type of dream they appear shifting and voluble. It is in this case of dream where the youth is presented to these shifting and voluble elements, that some time after his initiation, the one who made that particular rare dream becomes a shaman.

The initiatory dream is an experience that directly connects a human to a non-human, animal, plant, with its spirits, and visions of its deities. This world of singularity, unlike what we think to be the cosmos, is certainly not assured in itself to remain an eternal world. On the contrary, it is the responsibility of humans and shamans to ensure its balance, especially by knowing how to lead adequate sacrifice. Indeed, when we sacrifice, we do not only pay a tribute to ancestors or to the gods, we do not only recognize or acknowledge or celebrate a debt to the absolute that the world has set. The sacrifice maintains the very breath of the world, the very breath of the gods, the very flesh of the world, the very flesh of the gods. To sacrifice is to maintain the vital power of the world. Here man does not necessarily believe himself as detached from the world around him, such as the animal world. And even between men and animal there may be tender relations as Descola[9] mention about the Achuar from the Jivaro tribe.

In a shamanic society, if there is a specificity of the human being, that is to say, a maturity, the human being will find it in the essential task of being responsible for the balance of the world. It comes down to him to keep the world alive, as it is not written forever in a fixed secured form. The shaman is perpetually responsible bringing it alive while ensuring a good balance between different forces. Think of Tiresias' intervention towards Creon in the famous Greek myth. Tiresias comes to complain that the smoke of the offerings no longer rises to heaven, refused by the gods, since the sacrificed birds have fed from the dead body of Polynices, unburied by Royal Decree. This disorder portends the worst calamities, making Creon recant his decision, but too late.

The shaman works just like the shuttle of a weaver fabricating the world. He travels in both reverse and straight ways. He creates unexpected patterns, he produces singularities, where the cloth could pierce, tear out, weaken, break into pieces. For this he needs to journey with the permission to go on ecstatic trips to the kingdom of the dead, which he received in the very special

---

9 Philippe Descola, professo at « Collège de France », Dean of the Department of Nature Anthropology, he is the director of Social Anthropolohy Institute. He namely published « Les lances du crépuscule » relation Jivaros en Amazonie (Plon, 1993) and « Par-delà nature et culture » (Gallimard, 2005).

configuration that his dream gave him at the time of his initiation.

While he goes for a journey, the shaman lets himself be possessed, but not entirely. He remains partly lucid, which allows him to assume his mediator function. He has the responsibility to revive the colors of the world, to re-draw its contours, and to make it be heard when the humdrum of everyday life dulls it. The world could become unaware of this other realm, and the shaman's task is to prevent it from vanishing. Sophocles too falls into this same task of being the guardian of memory, of not forgetting the truth (Aletheia) when he explains that Colonus' prosperity will depend of the preservation of the memory of Oedipus' story.

The Art of Psychological Dissociation

Géza Roheim[10] puts his finger on something important about the skills of the shaman, which, for a novice, appear suspicious, or at least strange. He explains that during his trances, the shaman sometimes experiences spectacular states of psychological dissociation. Some troubled state could evoke schizophrenic symptoms, at least temporarily. One thing is certain; he who cannot dissociate is not a good shaman. We need to hear the dreams of these healers, their journey, the plurality of identities that inhabits them to understand their usefulness. Gullibly considering the "I" usually used as the proof of a unique identity is an error of judgment, a resistance. One should here recall the magisterial studies of Françoise Héritier on Samo identity (in Burkina Faso),

---

10 Géza Róheim is an American Ethnologist and Psychoanalyst from Hungary (1891-1953).

which says that the Samo members have seven organizations of personality, which he can highlight in turn, depending on the trade and negotiations which he must comply with, or the remedies which he wants or needs ...

A dissociated shaman is a shaman who offers an anthology of the living and of the dead. He is both a plurality of dead people and especially the one who revives what might mortify the life of the Gods ... if the balance of the debts and sacrifices that we owe them is not readjusted.

There are times, war, famine, epidemics major transgressions, where the human community can no longer maintain disjointed life and death. Then a shaman is required to redistribute the dividing lines between life and death, at the risk of a subjective death experience, and at the risk of representing a danger (when taken as a scapegoat) for the community after the balance has been restored. Jacques Galinier explains in "La moîtié du monde" [*Half of the World*] how in some African villages, once the shaman has done his job, the need or impulse to take a gun and shoot him down prevails. In case you may have a small temptation to become a shaman, remember that this is very difficult. You really have to go through some levels of examination, and I would much recommend Quebec rather than Mexico. But well, it depends, if you're suicidal, I would recommend you Mexico.

In "L'efficacité symbolique"[11], Levi-Strauss speaks of a Kuna people pregnant woman who cannot give birth. At the time of

---

[11] Lévi-Strauss Claude, "L'efficacité symbolique" In: Revue de l'histoire des religions, tome 135, n°1, 1949. pp. 5-27.

birth, the kid does not come out. So, a shaman woman stands at her bedside and tells a story where you see forces, you could say the Spirits, who will engage in a war. And this story is at once cosmological, political and somatic. Briefly, this is the war between the opening and closing forces.

The idea is that basically the shaman is fixing the body to operate again because she allowed the body to be projected and recomposed by following the thread of the epic narrated by herself, namely the victory of the opening forces over the closing forces.

Michel Perrin[12] realized that the words of the shaman in front of the patient, in this case the woman in labor who cannot let go of her child in the world, are articulated in a language no one understands. There is no idea that it is by hearing how her body will take the victory that it will be healed. This assumption is ruined; it does not work like that. The shamanic efficiency is not a narrative effectiveness; although it may well be that the musical game of the narrative of the Kuna shaman woman entails a crescendo of the opening over the closure through the musicality and energy of her speech. Again, one needs to better understand the position of the shaman that is to avoid the point of catastrophe, to separate the world of the living from that of death.

Levi-Strauss tells us repeatedly what this point of catastrophe could be, either in "The Jealous Potter", in "Introduction to a

---

12 Michel Perrin, born in 1941, is a French ethnologist and anthropologist, Research Director at the CNRS. He works at the Social Anthropology Laboratory (LAS) at the "College of France". He holds a Ph'd doctorate in physics, in Ethnology, in Humanities and he is an expert on shamanism. For nearly six years, he shared the lives of three American Indian populations.

Science of Mythology", "The Raw and the Cooked," "Naked Man" and "From Honey to Ashes." He raises the question of the nature of a myth. How does a mythological tale differ for example from an epic story, or from a fairytale? Is there any particular structure to a myth? This is where Levi-Strauss brings his structural analysis, which allows to associate the shamanic practice with the structure of a myth, to the extent that the latter also serves to separate death from life.

Myths and Shamanism

Indeed, the structure that is found in myths has the purpose of avoiding the coincidence of two extremes, two extreme points which are life of one side, and death on the other. The myth is what keeps the further apart life from death, the place where some opposition and transcendental potential are interspersed. Transcendence is intended to revive to the fertile and symbolic original unity. Doubtless it is here that shamanic-hermeneutics (like Sophocles, priest of Asclepius) differ from shaman-sorcerers. On the side of life, says Levi-Strauss, working on the myths of Quechua, we have agriculture, and near death, hunting. But agriculture itself stands between life and death but hunting too because one kills in order to eat. Farming and hunting are not only considered as economic activities, and not even just as survival activities. A small surplus is required each time, though not too much... But that overproduction cannot be harvested as something to capitalize on. It will either be destroyed ostentatiously before the chief of the nearby village or left to rot.

"One will leave the biggest yam rot on the village square. I saw that in Togo", Stéphane Breton[13] recounts in "La mascarade des sexes" in New Guinea. The surplus of the hunt will be offered, destroyed in a ceremonial way, agriculture on one side and hunting product on the other. The surplus of a certain balance between life and death cannot be capitalized. To break this balance would lead to the point of catastrophe, where life flows into death and inversely death into life. The symbolic effectiveness of the shaman is not limited to its therapeutic tools, but in the decisions he takes to avoid as much as possible reaching that point of catastrophe.

Hence the shaman seems as crazy as a myth might be in the eyes of a rational mind, and as wise as the messages conveyed by the myths, for those who do not stop at mere appearances. That's why the skills of the shaman for dissociation cannot be understood through the question of insanity as we are used to define it in the West. What matters is to seriously take the potential of the shaman, and to understand their necessities. In this, the shaman drums up that we live in an unstable world, with varying aspects, and that we are the weavers of this world.

Conclusion

Today the psychoanalyst, like the anthropologist, pays attention to broken transmission and to the effects of the history of violence on individuals as well as on communities. If the

---

13 Stéphane Breton, French filmmaker, ethnologist photographer. Ethnologist specialist of Melanesia, he is a member of the Laboratory of Social Anthropology at the "Collège de France", lecturer at the School for Advanced Studies in Social Sciences, teaches anthropology and documentary filmmaking.

anthropologist brings his or her attention to the new ideology of the identity, the psychoanalyst will more likely be willing to re-build for each the links that connect to ancestors and otherness. He will welcome and hear how each construct himself or herself as a real contemporary person. For the ones who come and talk to him, he may help to distinguish their dead and ghosts, to de-velop his grief, not to cut them off from his/her own lineages and foundations, but to study their particular histories and their uni-versality of complexes, by mean of which myth and history meet and weave new links.

Olivier Douville

Elisabeth Horowitz is a therapist specialized in Psychogenealogy and Brief Therapy. With a University background, and after years of practice in a private practice, she founded the *French Association of Psychogenealogy* in Paris (2001). She gives conferences and is the author of numerous books on personal development (see bibliography).

Her website: www.elisabeth-horowitz.com

3

Ten Primitive Rituals to Heal the Family Tree

Elisabeth Horowitz

If the very idea of analyzing the family tree or even to treat it is relatively recent (in the late nineteenth century with the beginnings of psychoanalysis), it nevertheless draws many of its concepts from the customs and rituals of the ancient societies. The concern to free oneself from transgenerational inheritance, which underlies many contemporary therapeutic approaches, is therefore not a new one as it refers far back to ancestral magical-religious practices.

For shamanic societies, the influences of the maternal and paternal lineages are real, and although we all know their famous "cult to the dead," their loyalty to the past and ancestors remains relative. Indeed, surprisingly, and whatever the continent (Oceania, Africa, Americas), many of their strategies are also especially designed to break free from the influence of family links.

In this article I will present ten "primitive" strategies chosen among all those that were observed and studied by anthropologists and famous thinkers (Sigmund Freud, Lucien Lévy-Bruhl, Claude Levi-Strauss). Then I will resume some of them for the purpose of a contemporary therapeutic application.

Frist strategy: a Totem as origin

In the West, our conception of the couple and of the family is overdetermined by an original model which is that of a first founding couple (Adam and Eve). Centuries of history demonstrate, if proof was needed, the devastating psychological impact of such a legend on couple relationships and on sexuality (tainted with shame) on countless generations. Native people are free from this. There is no mythical couple that can be higher than those they form or will form. No such story would limit them. And this is because the source of their lineage is not human, but totemic.

What is a totem? Specifically, it is an animal that is edible, harmless or dangerous and feared, more rarely a plant or a natural force (rain, water). The totem is, first of all, the group's ancestor. As non- human, from an alien race and therefore fundamentally different, it cannot represent an ideal for the men and women of a tribe and thus it cannot limit their intimate experience. Hence we can think that totemism offers greater freedom and softens family links because parenthood is not limited to all the members of a clan related by blood and/or alliance, but extends to (and ends with) anyone with a similar totem.

Those who have the same totem (falcon, frog, bison, etc.) are subject to the sacred obligation not to kill (or destroy) their totem and to abstain from eating its flesh. The totemic character is not inherent to any particular animal or to such other particular object (plant or natural force) but to all individuals belonging to the species of the totem. From time to time, festivals are celebrated for the members of the totemic group to reproduce or imitate, in ceremonial dances, the movements and characteristics of their totem.

One can assume that every member of the group knows that they cannot all be descendants of the totemic figure, but by pretending so, they evacuate the question of origins. If there is no human origin involved, no model prevails and the field of experience remains open. Shame, guilt, feelings of inferiority, forbidders and related quarrels disappear. Replaced by a Totem, the two founding human figures - Adam and Eve in our Western culture - who could emerge as superior to own descendants ("Grand male ancestor," "Great Grandmother" in Indigenous cultures), are absent. This significantly reduces the tension even within small family units.

Second strategy: changing names

To break free from family links and loyalties, a fine strategy used in ancient shamanic cultures is to avoid naming their parents, siblings and grandparents. In southern India, for example, women do not pronounce the name of their husbands, and in the Dakayo tribe, a man cannot utter the name of his parents-in-laws. Even the words that are phonetically similar to his family names cannot be pronounced.

Among the natives of the coast of Gacela Peninsula in New Britain, to pronounce the name of one's brother-in-law is very ill considered, just as in the Banks islands of Melanesia the prohibition to name people united by marriage is permanent. In Sulawesi, no words resembling the names of family members can be pronounced. If the father-in-law's name is Kallala, his son-in-law may not call a horse by its common name (Kawallo) and will be using a substitute word, Sasacajan (an animal to mount).

Long before the publication of the famous Sigmund Freud's opus entitled "Psychopathology of Everyday Life (1901)", the "primitive" knew that from the point of view of the unconscious, two words denoting different things but whose phonetics are similar or identical, are of equal value. They are, basically, the same word. By never saying the name of his parents and in-laws, the native symbolically extricate himself from the genealogical net in which he is caught (that of his family of origin and in-laws), and he thus retains a part of freedom. By changing the language, changing the names of his relatives, the indigenous emerges from a family system that set him at a fixed place and function.

This precaution also extends to the family members who died. Among the North American Indians, all the persons (men and women) with the same name as the one who just died are forced to abandon it and to adopt a new one. Sometimes, as with the tribes of the Rocky Mountains, this obligation only lasts during the mourning period, but on the Pacific coast, it is permanent. In conversations, syllables with the same resonance as the deceased's name are avoided. And if some are inadvertently spoken out, what do we they do? The inconsiderate call to the Dead is canceled by spitting thrice. This precaution also helps to untie the family group, to avoid repeating the same symptoms and to not be victim of identical circumstances of death.

When the name of a dead person is the same as - or synonymous to - an object of everyday life (water, fire, plant, animal, etc.), the latter it is immediately replaced. This custom takes place both in America and in Australia, and thereby the dialects regularly change and new words are created when required.

Thus, the Masaï in Africa have resorted to an ingenious additional method: changing the name of the deceased immediately after his/her death; from that moment, the deceased person could be named without fear, since all the prohibitions are related to his or her old name alone. In doing so, they assume that the spirit does not know the new name and won't be able to know who is being mentioned. The Australian tribes of the Adelaide and those of Encounter Bay push these precautions further: after a death, all those whose names were similar to that of the deceased person, have to take a new one.

In the tribe of Encounter Bay (Australia), if a man called Ngnke (water) dies, members of the clan will never use this term again, they have to create a new one to designate water. This also explains the large reserve of synonyms they have. One notices the same process among the Indians of Paraguay, where, when a word was once abolished, it cannot be used again. From one day to another, new words are born like mushrooms.

How to apply this strategy today? Is our name our destiny? Changing identity can be a powerful symbolic act, an express solution to difficult family inheritance issues and family abuse, such as bearing a parent's name or that of a deceased child or teenager, bearing the name of a family member guilty of violence or various abuse, that of the lover or mistress of one's father or mother, or being named after a fictional work (literary work or film), etc. Changing one's name or first name (or both) can redirect a destiny, and engage in much more positive ways.

Finally, as in certain risky situations undertaken by indigenous people (e.g., sea trip, forest expedition, long term trek) and during which no sensible word, least of all a relatives' name, is uttered, let's avoid mentioning family members during sensitive personal periods (a new relationship, a new job, career plans, trips, etc.).

Third strategy: freeing oneself from secrets

To most of us, psychoanalysis appears as a revolutionary civilization conquest of the twentieth century. For some part, this discipline has only rediscovered and expressed in new terms a conception of psychological and somatic disorders that probably goes back to the origins of mankind and which peoples we call primitive have not stopped using, often with skills that amaze our best practitioners. For indigenous people, a sick man (or his relatives in his place) will first have to "confess" some misconducts that may have been the cause of his illness – exactly as if were on the couch of a therapist.

According to shaman Inugpa Sugjuk, "people should not keep secrets". All the misdeeds that a man has tried to hide will grow bigger and become a living, fearsome evil if he does so. A secret is all the more harmful as it conceals an act that makes oneself impure - it then attracts a bad influence on its author and on those living near him. Such acts should therefore not be left ignored. On this condition alone can we stop their consequences. But it is not always sufficient. Furthermore, it is the author himself who has to avow the misdeeds. An unexpected, inexplicable misfortune suddenly reveals that an influence is exercised on those it strikes and that they are impure. How did they become so? Perhaps through their own fault, without their knowing it. Maybe because of one of them, and his misdeeds have tainted the entire group, attracting misfortune upon them all.

To stop this situation, which threatens to be fatal, and for the group to become pure again, there is an indispensable preliminary condition. It is necessary that the person who contracted the soiling admits his fault. Confession is required. As long as it did not take place, the consequences of the soiling continues to expend. Some examples should shed more light on these principles.

The wife of a native missionary returned from New Guinea to her family in Fiji. She got on board on a cutter, in Sawa, with her little boy. Shortly after the start, a storm broke out and the waves began to wash over the boat. A larger wash of water reached the child and hurled him into the sea. The captain, with great courage, threw himself into the moving waters to save the child. He managed to reach him, but the strong wind prevented the sailors to bring the boat close enough. Then a huge shark approached them. Horrified, the captain expected to be seized at every moment, so he continued struggling in the waves ... It took a while for the boat to manage to save them. No sooner had the captain set foot on board, glaring around at the crew and passengers, almost like a judge, that he asked: "Who is the cause for that?"

Then, the child's mother prostrated herself on the deck and confessed the crime she had committed in New Guinea before leaving. Immediately, all the people on board felt relieved, considering that what had happened was completely explained and that it could not have been avoided, given the circumstances.

In a similar vein, before starting a battle, an entire confession for one's sins is asked to warriors, generally in public. This is a very common practice in primitive tribes or even in quite developed societies: it was found in Indonesia, in Polynesia, among the Eskimos, in Mexico, in Peru at the age of the Inca, in the Bantu tribes in Africa, and even elsewhere. In Samoa, before going into battle, the warriors are sprayed with coconut water, and each of them confesses all the sins he may have been guilty of and, having been sprayed, he generally pronounces a prayer to obtain protection and success.

Another variant? Men make as many knots (as admitted mistakes) on a rope, which they then burn to free themselves. These same Samoans recognize of high value a confession made in case of danger - on sea, the helmsman steers the boat against the wind and then all the men confess their past abuse. One said, "Well, I stole a fowl in such a village"; another admits to having sinned with a married woman in another village, etc. After the men, each in his turn, have made their confessions or claimed their innocence, the boat takes the wind again and they feel sure that the crew will stay safe during the crossing.

If the consequences of some mistakes may rain down upon others and on a group, this is a fortiori the case between members of the same family and between generations. The sins of ancestors (such as extramarital affairs, illegitimate children, homosexuality or bisexuality, sexual abuse, incest, adoptions, violence, etc.) are thus passed on to the next generations. The consequences are often heavy (melancholy, depression, fear, failure syndrome, unconscious repetition of ignored facts).

Thus, in shamanic primitive societies, in case of sickness, a common use is to call each and every one to confess what mistake they might have committed. The use of confession, whether in private or in public, is almost mandatory, be it in Indonesia, Polynesia, Mexico, Africa or in the Arctic regions. As long as a fault is kept secret, its influence appears insidious. In Samoa, in case of serious illness, the high priest of the village asks the patient's friends to bring his family and make a confession.

Indeed, natives know that a health problem may also be the consequence of genealogical secrets. Those concerning the lineage are in the front line (one's father's and mother's or siblings' identities) and seem to have an influence on the metabolism and the immune system. And what if what is happening in the family cell could induce mutations in the other cells (the body's)?

Fourth strategy: Prohibiting incest

In all shamanic cultures, as in contemporary societies, incest is a major taboo. Uniting with his one's fellows, that is to say to with a man or woman belonging to one's family group, is not without causing serious consequences. Without the ban that prohibits it, everyone would have relationships with relatives and no exchange with the outside would be possible.

We have to add a number of customs, meant to prevent individual sex between close relatives, which are rigorously observed, just as they are in our Western culture.

In the peninsula of Gazelles in New Britain, a sister, once married, must not speak to her brother; instead of pronouncing his name, she must refer to him by a circumlocution. In New Mecklenburg, the same prohibition applies not only between siblings, but also between cousins. They must not come close to each other, or shake hands, nor give each other's gifts; when they want to speak to one another, they must do so at a distance of few steps.

In the Bettas, in Sumatra, prohibitions extend to all sorts of relatives. In the Barongo tribe of the Delagoa Bay, in Africa, the most stringent precautions are imposed on men in regard to their relations to their sisters-in- law. When a man comes across his sister-in-law somewhere, as she is dangerous for him, he carefully avoids her. He daren't eat in the same dish as hers, he cannot speak to her without trembling, he has difficulty approaching her hut, and he greets her with a barely audible voice.

In the Banko islands, these prohibitions are very severe and of a cruel strictness. A man and his mother-in-law should avoid being near one another. When, by chance, they meet on a path, the mother-in-law must step aside and turn her back on her son-in-law until he has gone, or vice versa. At Vanna Lava (Port Patterson), a son-in-law does not set foot on the beach after the passing of his mother-in-law before the tide has wiped her footsteps from the sand. They have to talk at a distance away, and it is understood that they should not pronounce one another's names.

Despite this timeless and universal prohibition, incestuous impulses that lead you to cherish your first love objects (your parents, grandparents, siblings or cousins) sometimes remain strong after childhood and teenage years. For if you can easily detach from relationships that satisfied and fulfilled you, you cannot do so when the vital need to be loved and recognized has remained frustrated and therefore unfulfilled.

How do we know that this drive towards parents (originally natural and spontaneous) has crystallized? When we spend time with people or love people who have similar names as our parents, who in some cases are doing the same job, have a significant age and / or have a similar date of birth (or a similar address).

How does this apply today? In his book "Totem and Taboo" (1912), Freud says that in the Fiji Island, the prohibition of incest is particularly stringent; it concerns not only blood relatives, but also brothers' and sisters' groups. We are even more surprised to learn that these savages have sacred orgies, during which they precisely fulfill the most prohibited sexual unions. They act out their incestuous impulse in a specific situation and for a limited time.

On the same principle, the simplest act is to create a mask from the photograph of a parent (or both) and wear it, or make it wear to one's spouse during the act of love and say their names when reaching the orgasm. Hence it metaphorically enacts the unconscious desire of the sexual act with the parents.

Finally, in his book "The ceremony of Naven" (1935), ethnologist and future founder of the school of Palo Alto Gregory Bateson says that some tribes regularly dress-up: men dress up as women and vice versa. This ritual can also be used for cathartic purpose (e.g., when you are a boy and your parents have always wanted a girl, it is possible, for example, to dress up as a girl part of the day and this for as many days as your age number. You will burn the clothes afterwards).

Fith strategy: Miniaturizing the familial links

Another method is to create miniature family situations to repair some delicate relations between spouses and /or between parents and their children. In New Caledonia, the people shape miniature effigies of the tribe's members to maintain or restore harmony between men and women. To that end, they firmly tie up all their little figurines together to ensure the consistency and strength of their love.

In a tribe of South India, small naked male and female wooden statuettes are manufactured in Tirupati to be sold to Hindus. Those who are childless celebrate an ear piercing ceremony on these statuettes, believing that some posterity will come as a consequence. Or, if in a family, there still are single boys or girls, their parents celebrate the wedding ceremony between two dolls, hoping that the marriage of their children will soon follow. They dress the dolls, put jewelry on them, and a true marriage ceremony takes place. There are people who, for a doll wedding, spend as much money as for a real marriage. In the mind of these Hindus, prefiguring the happy event with miniatures will have the effect of making it happen.

How to apply this strategy today? Psychologically, a miniaturized (or larger) image can help to free oneself from difficult situations. How to proceed?

Miniaturizing a frightening family situation: Like the fisherman who mimed in advance his departure at sea using miniatures, you can make small figurines that will help you to represent a situation that seems difficult to live. Miniaturization allows for better control. Once reduced in size, this one seems less frightening. To a client uncomfortable at her family gatherings, I advised to miniaturize the whole scene before going there, which allowed her to master her fears and to regain her confidence.

Reducing parental influence: To Sophie, a client dominated by her parents (a very possessive mother, a rigid and authoritarian father) I advised to enlarge their photos at a maximum size (that of a giant poster) and then, every day, to reduce their size by using smaller and smaller copies until she reached a miniature version the size of a postage stamp. On a symbolic level, you increase the parental power (amplification) in order to better decrease it. Thus reduced, the parents' images, and what they represent, lose their threatening power, becoming more neutral, and eventually harmless.

Sixth strategy: anticipating the family program

If an Indian sees the warning signs of adverse events (for example, a striking dream most probably prophetic , in which his house is burning), he will not wait for it to happen for real: the very next day he will put on a performance what he saw and light the fire to a small hut built expressly for that purpose. This way, the action of the event to come is no longer to be feared. It was exhausted by this anticipation. One will set up, more or less completely, the opposite event to the one that is felt imminent. For example, if you see yourself hit by a misfortune in a dream, once awake, the dream will be put on a performance as soon as possible and in the best possible way.

That way, you substitute a symbolic equivalent to a threatening fate. You make it real in advance, and so you're even: It has already taken place; therefore, it will not happen again. Among the Indians of New France, a man dreamed that he was captured by the enemy and tortured as usual; the next day he got tied up to a post by his friends, and he asked them to pretend to inflict him cruel injuries. To do so, one of them traced big red lines on his skin.

How to apply this strategy today? In the same vein, imagine your family has made predictions and has programmed for you to live difficult situations: "You'll end up in poverty on the streets," "In our family (you as well), everyone dies young ' "On our side, women always outlive their husbands," "Artists all end up on the streets," etc.

How to solve this? Apply the same process and enact the family prediction through a symbolic act: dress up as a bum and go begging in the streets a number of days equivalents to your age number. You can also print business cards with the mention, under your name, "deceased" early/ in his twentieth year" (at any rate an age younger than your real one) before handing them out in a crowded street or putting them in mailboxes in the neighborhood. The words can be changed by "X Widow or widower Y ...." The fear of having an accident, as other family members had, may also be enacted, for example by sleeping in a car after having been painted with several liters of artificial blood and by having snapshots of the scene taken. This way, the negative prediction is exhausted in advance, as it was carried out before it could occur.

Seventh's strategy: freeing oneself from hostile drives

Some tribes do not just draw a portrait or even make a small object imitating the original; they create a full height carved mannequin in wax or with straws. This is the case with the caciques tribes in South America; they create a mannequin representing their enemy, feign to engage in combat with him, and cover him with injuries before cutting him into pieces. Thus, they symbolically unload their hostile impulses and anger.

How to apply this strategy today? We know that the family of origin is far from being unconditionally favorable to life and it is sometimes urgent to break free from deep problems, when the parents and ancestors were not an instrument in their descendants' emotional, physical or occupational success, but to the very reason for their failure.

The more important are the abuse (e.g., constant criticism, repeated verbal abuse, corporal punishment, indifference, possessiveness, preference for other children in the home, shelving side-lining, "scapegoat" child, refusal that the child express his vocation and do job he likes, etc.), the greater the resentment is the greater is the secret desire to be free from the oppressive parents, even in to the point of revenge, although these drives are usually minimized and denied, that is to say repressed. To counter this on a symbolic level, one will cut into pieces a mannequin whose face will have previously been pasted with the photograph of the offending parent.

Eighth strategy: expelling the genealogical pathology

Do you remember the famous request by Sigmund Freud to his patients with a symptom? "Who are you trying to imitate?" Who, in the family before you, had the same affliction? In other words, who do you unconsciously seek to mimic? Limitation is at the origin of many symptoms, as we know that many of the descendants are trying to gain their parents' or ancestors' love by identifying to them on the physical level.

In indigenous communities, the medicine-man does not need, like our practitioners, to carefully examine the patient, to think of interpreting the symptoms and to bring out a diagnosis in the medical sense of the word. At the most, the patient's appearance could make him think of a prognosis he will keep for himself (infections, viruses, bacteria, family secrets and conflicts, evil spirit are synonymous in his eyes). The disease being a materialized impurity, the medicine-man will treat it with a spectacular technique. He first conducts a vigorous massage of the whole body or of the parts where the evil seems to have taken refuge; he kneads those parts with great effort, often for hours, to compel the cause of evil to move under the skin to a certain spot, and then he rubs or sucks on the parts. He finally extracts a small object - a stone, a rod, a sheet, a spine, a bone fragment, a worm, an insect - which is the visible form of the disease. What is extracted with so great a difficulty from the patient's body sometimes comes out of the mouth of the healer. In those cases he had taken care to place it there before starting the treatment.

To achieve this, as Claude Lévi-Strauss was able to describe it, the caregiver performs a symbolic action, prefiguring the desired expulsion of the evil. He performs beforehand what is going to happen when it takes place. He therefore acts as if he triumphed over the resistance of the evil principle by energetic and prolonged sucking efforts, and finally managed to retrieve the object that materialized its presence.

Though the medicine-man only pretends to withdraw iron spikes out of the body of his patient by sucking and spitting them in his hand, the natives sees it and believes in the process. It seems they are not fooled by the trickery, and yet they claim that the ceremony produces the expected effect. They have of what is going on a different idea from ours ... To them, it's just a symbolic action. But it entails representations of both the desired effect and that of the ceremony, combined in one, and seems as effective as a real surgery.

Other medicine-men will, for their parts, perform real operations to examine the internal organs and take out the cause of evil with a knife. The famous anthropologist W. Bogoras attended one such operation on a young boy of fourteen totally naked; his mother, a shaman, opened his belly and you could see the blood and the open wound. She deeply plunged her hand in the wound and then the flesh healed without leaving a trace. He saw another shaman opening his own abdomen.

How to use this strategy today? For all the situations that refer to an identification to the parents, to their symptoms and diseases, sometimes at the same age, the symbolic act will be to write the parent's name on a sticker and to put it on the body part or on the concerned organ, to leave it for a specific number of days before taking it off, and thereby freeing the patient from the mimetic impulse. One can also make use of placebo operations: it implies pretending to open the body and remove the evil in the form of a mass or of a small object.

One may also imitate an integral operation. The principle is more than interesting: true or false, if magic can heal, one can then perform placebo operations that the unconscious will take for real. For example, in case of a tumor, apply an octopus that symbolizes it on the diseased part of the body and then pretend to detach the octopus/tumor with great effort or use a huge knife to perform an imaginary surgery or even pretend to "replace" the organs. It is the principle of operation in itself that is impressive and seems to have a transmuting power on the unconscious.

Ninth strategy: using masks

At the New Hebrides, as well as in Africa and throughout the Pacific, there are distinctive masks used in ceremonies of secret societies, which are quite different from usual masks. With the initiation mask, comes a costume made of leaves that completely hides the wearer. The goal is to 'erase' one's personality, and one's genealogical ties, so that the "Great Spirit" can manifest itself. In a more common way, masks also serve as mediators and express many liberating emotions in regard to relatives. Sober or feathered, laughing or terrifying, fitting the face or of vertiginous dimensions, monochrome or colorful, their vivid expressions illustrate the full range of moods and human feelings.

How to apply this strategy today? As at the theater, and to free yourself from genealogical influences, you can easily make a mask - or more - with the photographs of family members' faces, primarily your parents, siblings, uncles and aunts, insofar as you still feel under their influence and / or identified to them.

You will go to a public place for an hour, wearing the mask of your mother's face, then the next that of day your father's, then the day after that of your brother's or sister's (especially if they were dominant because preferred). Then you will burn them.

To solve a more ancient conflict and have an ultimate explanation (with a deceased person for instance), you will create a mask on which will be pasted the person's photograph. You will then ask a theater student -whom you pay for the service- to wear the mask and the same clothes – or similar ones- as those of the parent you want to have an explanation with. You then will address the 'surrogate' parent as if he were the parent indeed and express your feelings. This works because the subconscious gives to symbols and metaphors the same value as to real facts.

Tenth strategy: eating the earth of origin

Yesterday as today, and for every family, having to leave one's land, one's region or country is a major trauma that often has tragic consequences, since breaking the links with the original land will often induce a reshuffling of blood links on the short term. An indigenous cannot leave his local group to be naturalized or adopted by another group. As the land is his, he belongs to his land. If he leaves, he becomes a foreigner ... Today most of the lands belong to the White, and the indigenous have to live wherever it is possible for them. But whatever the situation in our 'modern' world is, the attachment of a man to his land and to his local group remains alive.

There is an effective African symbolic rite that shows the importance of the relationship between the land and the group that lives there: when a Ronga comes back from Kimberley with the woman he married there, they bring back a small amount of earth taken from the place they just left, and the woman has to eat a little of it every day in her soup, to get used to her new home. This chunk of earth softens the transition between the two homes.

How to apply this strategy today? For a family, besides changing social class, leaving one's region or country or immigrating to another continent, is the most important source of post-traumatic stress. Indeed, the soil provides continuity, a consistency that human relations alone cannot guarantee. Soil loss is often experienced as a personal wound which will always speak, decades later, to many expatriates. To avoid these effects, simply have a chunk of earth from your place of origin and absorb a few grams every day as a symbolic act.

To conclude

Towards a neo-shamanism? By opening a window on humanity as it still was yesterday, relatively intact and unchanged in remote areas until the mid-twentieth century, I hope I have been able to offer throughout these pages, a first panoramic view of the opportunities for change and healing offered by the enactment of symbolic acts. All are inspired by original and creative solutions from the various 'primitive' tribes populating the five continents.

As a therapist, everyday experience makes me believe that besides the word and its many therapeutically virtues, mini rituals, placed strategically, also allow emerging successfully from transgenerational influences.

Bibliography of the Author

Élisabeth Horowitz (2000), *Se libérer du destin familial*, Éditions Dervy, Paris.

Élisabeth Horowitz (2002), *Se libérer du temps généalogique*, Éditions Dervy, Paris.

Élisabeth Horowitz (2003), *Sous l'influence du destin familial*, Éditions Dervy, Paris.

Élisabeth Horowitz (2004), *La maladie, une mémoire généalogique*, Éditions Dervy, Paris.

Élisabeth Horowitz (2005), *Les fantômes du passé*, Éditions Dervy, Paris.

Élisabeth Horowitz (2006), *L'enfant et l'arbre généalogique*, Éditions Dervy, Paris.

Élisabeth Horowitz (2008), *Derniers soupirs, grands secrets*, Robert Laffont, Paris.

Élisabeth Horowitz (2011), *Freud express*, Albin Michel, Paris.

Élisabeth Horowitz (2012), *La Psychogénéalogie*, Ixelles Éditions, Bruxelles.

Élisabeth Horowitz (2012), *Les nouveaux secrets de famille*, Ixelles Éditions, Bruxelles.

Élisabeth Horowitz (2013), *La Chronogénéalogie*, Éditions Hachette, Paris.

Élisabeth Horowitz (2014), *Les actes libérateurs*, Éditions Dervy, Paris.

Élisabeth Horowitz (2015), *Les actes symboliques*, Éditions Jouence, Genève.

Élisabeth Horowitz (2015), *Le transgénérationnel dans la vie des célébrités*, ouvrage collectif, Écodition, Genève.

Élisabeth Horowitz (2015), *Pratiquer la pensée sauvage*, Éditions Dervy, Paris.

Myron Eshowsky, M.S., Counseling Psychology, is a counselor, shamanic healer, and educator. He is co-developer of the Social Health Care Program for Syrian Refugees, which provides direct services and training in trauma treatment for refugees within the Middle East. Between 1987 and 1994, he worked in a community mental health center specifically as a shamanic healer. He has brought shamanic work to prisons, hospitals, social service agencies working with youth at risk, and mental health centers. He has published dozens of articles on these topics in professional journals and his book, *Peace with Cancer: Shamanism as a Spiritual Approach to Healing.*

For the last thirty years, he has studied extensively how indigenous cultures address the healing of trauma and conflict. He consults and teaches throughout the United States, Canada, Africa, the Middle East, and Europe.

Website: www.myroneshowsky.com

4
History That Never Ends: Healing Transgenerational Trauma in Community Life

Myron Eshowsky

Historically, shamans have been viewed as mediators between the life of the ordinary world and the extraordinary world of the spirits. Beyond being healers of disease, their concern with restoring balance and harmony to the collective soul of the group reminds us of the critical role shamans play in community life. In that perspective, history is not seen as something of the past, but rather as something that is very much alive within us and around us. In fact, shamans have always addressed history and transgenerational issues to bring harmony or healing.

Introduction

This chapter explores elements of shamanic world-views and by extension, a shamanistic approach to transgenerational trauma and healing through the use of ritual and ceremony. As Schirch[1] has noticed, indigenous societies "seem to prefer symbols and rituals of communication as opposed to Western industrial societies, which prefer more direct communication modes," the advantage of the former being that transgenerational healing often takes shape as full-sensory experiential shifts in

---

[1] Schirch, Lisa (2005), *Ritual and Symbol in Peacebuilding*, Kumarian Press, Bloomfield, CT.

community and individual consciousness to bring spiritual resolve, whereas words alone may only scratch the surface.

The rituals often make history visible where it has been secret,
hidden, denied, or invisible to our knowing. To transcend and
heal our inheritance of generations of trauma, we must first be
made conscious of them. By their nature these rituals are transformative. They challenge and change the status quo. Symbolically, they become a rite of passage toward a new vision, a new
set of values, or a new structure in community life. And in becoming conscious, we are able to make clear choices and take
actions to honor the lessons of the past and move into a new
dream for the future generations. In this way, we live the Native
axiom, "Heal seven generations back, and connect our actions of
today for the seven generations forward." With consciousness of
these inherited wounds, there is thus agency to heal them for-
wards and backwards.

Ritual can influence people's emotions and thoughts through
the power of symbols, the language too, of dream and the conscious alive world in which we live. The metaphors dans meanings inherent in ritualistic healing works essentially cracks us
open as individuals to be bigger, communal story, or drama, unfolding. Trauma experts such as Peter Levine, Bessel van der
Kolk, David Berceli and others remind us that traumatic experiences are stored in our bodies and senses. These experiences are
often beyond our capacity to describe in words. The indigenous
view is that humans communicate in ritual primarily through
their bodies, senses, and emotions rather than words. It is as
Paula Gunn Allen describes in her book The Sacred Hoop, Native ritual "transforms something from one state or condition to

another."[2] As she shares: "The distractions of ordinary life must be put to rest and emotions redirected and integrated into a ceremonial context so that the greater awareness can come into full consciousness and functioning. In this way the participants become literally one with the universe, for they lose consciousness of mere individuality and share the consciousness that characterizes most orders of being...Soon breath, heartbeat, thought, emotion, and word are one."

The Shamanic worldview

The following elements characterize a shamanistic approach to healing transgenerational trauma:

1. All parts of the world are interconnected, on all levels of reality, from the physical to the spiritual; whatever happens to one individual affects all others, and whatever happens to others affects the individual.

2. The objects perceptible to human senses are local manifestations of larger patterns of energy.

3. That which is imperceptible to human senses is as important in illness as that which can be measured and validated through the senses.

4. Consciousness is all-pervasive, or in other words, "everything is alive."

---

[2] Gunn Allen, Paula (1992), *The Sacred Hoop: Recovering the Feminine in American Indian Traditions*, Beacon Press, Boston (MA), p. 80

5. The universe as a whole is sacred and has purpose and meaning.[3]

A shamanic worldview informs us that the unhealed stories of the ancestral past which exist in the spiritual realms are very much alive as agents of illness and conflict within the community. We pay the debts of the past. If we have not cleared the slate, an invisible ancestrally loyalty impels us to repeat a moment of incredible joy or unbearable sorrow, an injustice, or a tragic death. Shamanic mediation of these unhealed traumas offers the living - and the dead – an opportunity to shift these inherited legacies through ritual and healing on a communal scale.

Unlike Western psychology, which tends to view transgenerational trauma as an individual response, shamans view the effects of trauma as a collective experience needing symbolic group healing and purification rituals. Additionally, the spiritual effects of trauma are seen as transcending time space and time. In Africa, the realm of the ancestors is a world parallel to this one and is also the realm of the unborn; birth and death shoulder each other in the circle, or "sacred hoop" of life. It is where our fate, our deepest sense of meaning is determined before our birth. Initiation involves crossing the river to that timeless place to remember our original purpose. Transgenerational trauma is viewed as the responsibility of all of us to heal so the ancestors may be freed from that which was left unresolved at the time of their deaths.

---

[3] Mehl-Madrona, Lewis (1998), *Coyote Medicine: Lessons from Native American Healing*, Simon and Schuster Press, NY.

Sometimes, ancestral legacies in need of healing are bound up in spiritual landscapes of physical ones. Going beneath the surface, the spirit of a place holds the context of history waiting to be healed. It remains important to understand that a shamanic view of transgenerational trauma is seen as a "soul wound", a trauma that occurred in the soul or spirit of both the individual and the collective. All forms of sickness and healing are seen as spiritual.

Toni Morrison fleshes out this parallel world in her book *Beloved*, as one of the narrators, Sethe, tries to explain to her daughter Denver that even if emancipation has happened in historical time, in the spirit world, the plantation is still present and unchanged: "Some things you forget. Other things you never do... Places, places are still there. If a house burns down, it's gone, but the place - the picture of it - stays, and not just my memory, but out there, in the world. What I remember is a picture floating around out there outside my head. I mean, even if I don't think it, even if I die, the picture of what I did, or knew, or saw is still out there right in the place where it happened... Where I was before I came here, that place is real. It's never going away. Even if the whole farm - every tree and grass blade of it dies."[4] Places, like the beds of rocks on which they rest, are layered and ever-dreaming the memories of all time; all-present.

To understand how unhealed or non-integrated histories are transmitted over time and generation, it is helpful to use simple categories put together by anthropologist Frank Clements[5] who

---

[4] Morisson, Toni (1987), *Beloved*, Alfred Knopf, NY, p. 36.
[5] Clements F.E., (1932), *Primitive concepts of disease*, University of California, Archeology and Ethnography, 32, p. 85-252.

worked extensively with Native peoples. Conceptually, breaking the cycle of transmission can be distilled into 1) the removal of something which does not belong (i.e. object or spirit intrusion), and/or 2) the restoration of something which should be there and has gone missing (i.e. soul parts.) These categories of transmission include:

Object intrusion: The belief that an object has intruded into the body. The object can invade the body by some random event, or it can be placed there by someone wanting to cause suffering. Therapy for this type of illness is removal of the object by extracting it through cutting, bleeding, or sucking.

Loss of soul: The belief that one's soul has been lost. This can easily be understood as a depersonalization in which the person may have lost contact with reality.

Spirit intrusion: The belief that illness is caused by an outside entity invading the personality. Relevance can be found in the Western concept of multiple personality disorder.

Breech of taboo: Illness due to the guilt caused when an individual violates a societal rule.

Sorcery: Illness that occurs if someone with power willfully inflicts physical, psychological, or spiritual illness on an individual.

In this worldview, the dark side of history repeats itself as long as the unhealed factors of the past remain present. As Morrison alludes in her fiction, it is true that these repeating patterns may be contained in a place in our known reality. A good example of that comes from the Kosovo area. Before it was the site of the recent Balkan conflicts as Yugoslavia dissolved, it was the site for the start of World War I. And earlier yet, during the Middle Ages, Ottomans (Muslims Turks) and Serbs (Christians, Orthodox) fought for leadership in the Balkans. The Battle of Kosovo Fields in 1389 ended on June 28 of that year with the defeat of the Serbs by the Ottomans. And it was on the anniversary of this defeat, that a Serbian activist killed Archduke Franz Ferdinand in 1914 for the perceived humiliation of Serbia - which changes the whole geopolitics of Europe. And, strikingly enough, it was on that same date in 1989, the 600th anniversary of the Battle of Kossovo Fields, that Slobodan Milosevic, president of Serbia, invokes the Battle of Kosovo to call Serbs to arms in the Balkan conflicts in his speech: "Never again will Islam subjugate the Serbs." Curiously or not, to the day in 2001, the Government of Serbia flew the former president out of his resident country to The Hague in the Netherlands to stand trial for crimes against humanity and war crimes, supported by an international arrest warrant issued by the United Nations. As the adage goes, history repeats itself - traumas incubated in time and place that self-perpetuate until healing shifts the trajectory.

An unhealed collective history of a people may also express itself as conflict amongst various tribal, racial, religious, or ethnic groups. For example, Black men in the United Sates may experiment prison as the frontlines of spiritual warfare, for it is in prison that Black Americans may return most completely to the hold of the slave ship. It can become the spiritual trial that either transforms them or devours their soul.

The case studies below will further illustrate how unhealed history may express itself in places, groups, or individuals and how shamanic healing and ritual work can increasingly restore peace and harmony from the individual on up to a community scale.

Communal Trauma Healing Stories

1. Drama on Traumatized Land

The aftermath of serial killer Jeffrey Dahmer, also known as "The Milwaukee Cannibal", left dozens of family members and neighborhood people with profound shame and grief. His acts of sexual perversity, macabre dismemberment, and killings at his Wisconsin haunts received international attention. After his arrest, the Oxford apartment building where his later killings occurred was torn down by the City of Milwaukee in 1992. In the spring of 2000, an ecumenical healing ritual was organized to memorialize and heal the wounds still gaping on the grounds of that place.

People in the neighborhood were hoping for some kind of spiritual service to help bring healing and restore vitality to the surrounding neighborhood. At first, the local neighborhood association embraced the idea of an openly performed ecumenical service, but later asked that the service not be performed as a public event for fear that public attention would bring more shame to the neighborhood.

In my preparatory shamanic journeys, the spirits presented the problem as a place with too much fire and that water was needed to bless the land. The journey peeled back the history of the land to a time pre-dating Dahmer: the souls of many dead Native people still lingered on this site. When the time for the ceremony came, none of the ministers expected to come did so, except for one Catholic priest, Father Paul. The two of us were left to orchestrate the ritual. Not knowing what he could offer, I suggested that he bless the land with water.

When we arrived, the sense of death at the site was overwhelming. The lot was devoid of any living plant life. A dead tree and dried out weeds filled the lot along with concrete rubble and stones. Nothing there was alive. Spiritually I sensed many ghosts there and I could hear the Native American ghosts repeatedly saying, "Bring us peace, bring us peace!" Neighborhood people, family members whose loved ones were murdered by Dahmer, and other community people had gathered by then to bring healing to this place. As I invoked the circle, I asked all to speak from their hearts. Many tears flowed. This crying was the water of healing for this land, an honoring and remembrance of the lives lost. As people shared their grief, their shame, and their prayers for healing, more people from the area continued to come out to watch. They came up and thanked us for what we were doing and eventually asked if they could join in, and they did.

After Father Paul blessed the land with water, each person was given water and seeds to offer as healing for this place. Meanwhile, I stood in the middle of the rubble and conducted souls of the discarnate spirits to the upper realms. In the midst of all this, a history teacher who lived in the neighborhood shared a story with me that revealed a different slant to the reason of why we were there, an extrapolation of the hints presented in my preparatory journeys by the presences of the Native American spirits trapped in this earthly realm.

The teacher told me, "This place in Milwaukee is the highest point in the city. In the old days, the native people of the area would meet here to hold peace ceremonies when there were conflicts. In the early 1800's, during one of these peace councils,

U.S. troops massacred hundreds who had gathered." It was the site of a mass killing. Later, an apartment building was built there - the building in which Dahmer would live, and where many of his victims would die. As this history teacher explained, the Native view was that the place had become a place of massacre, until it was fully healed. After he told this story, we led ceremony to pray for the dead spirits trapped there, asking that their suffering end and they be released from the earth. Everyone there was given tobacco to make this prayer in their own way and give the tobacco to the land.

This healing ceremony shows how much ancient non-integrated events can create a "place spirit" that influences similar stories to take place again and again. It was important to connect with the roots of the problem (the massacre of the Native, in this case) to not only provide some explanation to the drama that one person played out, but to also prevents theses historical violence from repeating.

2. Reconnecting His Grandfather

Through a grant, teenagers from around the world were invited to participate in an international youth peace conference that ran concurrently with an annual international conference in conflict resolution held in St. Petersburg, Russia. Those attending from the United States travelled from some of the country's most torn areas: gang members from South Central Los Angeles, and Native youth from pueblos in New Mexico. Internationally, there were also youth from Israel/ Palestine, Africa, India, and China.

One Native youth particularly stood out. He wore an oversized hoodie that hid his face. Inside or out, he always wore sunglasses, and he was constantly writing in a notebook. I knew he was watching me and taking in the training offered in shamanic approaches to peacemaking and healing. After several days, he approached me, asking for healing work. Ray (pseudonym) was in heroin withdrawal and had come to the conference without telling anyone what was occurring for him. He had been hiding his physical distress by covering up. I told him we would need big group energy for a healing ritual and he agreed to my asking other youths to join us.

In a midnight healing ceremony, about 75 youths joined us to help drum and witness the ceremony. It was explained to them that I would be extracting the heroin spirit and dancing it in my own body until it agreed to leave. The instruction was to avoid looking at me while I was dancing the heroin spirit. The spirit of heroin presented itself as a rattling skeleton, what I would call a "death spirit" for it was eating his life force. Several of the youths later described hearing the rattling sounds of the bones.

Once the heroin spirit was extracted, it came out as a dance that I started to have with Ray. He danced with me while the drumming continued. The heroin spirit had filled a large hole of soul loss within Ray, and a traditional healing journey to restore his soul was conducted. Then I began to show him the dance and he began shaking in a spiritual way. Quickly we began what he later told me was the Thunderbird dance taught to him by his grandfather when he was a little boy. As the drumming intensified, he had the feeling of flying around the room. It went on for hours.

Later, Ray shared with all of us that he saw his grandfather's spirit in the circle. He began to cry and talk about how the traditions he learned as a little one had died off and his family had broken apart through drugs and alcohol. He shared stories of his ancestors having been taken away from their families to live at the Indian schools. There they were forbidden to practice their culture or speak their language. His father has been in the military and when he came back he was not the same. He remembered little of his father, only knowing stories of his drinking and violence. His father abandoned the family when he was about five years old. His grandfather's spirit told him the "dance would heal him and some of the past hurts of the tribe to restore his people."

Prior to the healing ceremony, Ray had rejected traditional culture, and in his return to the U.S., he made some effort to learn more of what his grandfather had tried to teach him. I stayed in contact with Ray for a few years. He remained drug-free, finished high school, and was enrolled in college to become a writer/storyteller.

3. The Bear Ancestor

I received a call from a Ho Chunk Nation elder, Tom, asking if I would be willing to come up and do a place healing ceremony for some land the tribe had purchased to raise buffalo and horses. The intent of the tribe was to have teenage youth work to care for the animals and for tribal spiritual leaders to teach them traditional ceremonies. For some reason, nothing was working right on the land and he had heard I was doing healing work with places. I asked him who would be there and he said, "A couple of us elders and about 10 teenagers."

As I drove up on our agreed upon day, a little voice in my head told me I was to do the whole ceremony in Hebrew. When I got to the place, I saw that this had been a former horse farm and was quite large. When I entered the farm building, it was full with about 300 adults and another 20 or so teenagers. As is often the case, word had traveled amongst the tribe via what was jokingly called "Indian telegraph". People showed up to support the ceremony for the land and the efforts to work with the young people. A large circle of chairs set the sacred stage for our gathering.

I was asked by Tom to tell about how I learned to work with the spirits and what we would be doing. Being on the receiving end of violence throughout my childhood because I was Jewish, I spent a lot of time alone outdoors. During that time, I would sit in a circle of giant oak trees, drumming the black earth until spirits would come to talk with me. I had learned how to connect this way from my great aunt, a "dreaming woman" and healer. She would ask me about what I learned from the spirits and we would "dream" together. She had taught me that places hold history of what had happened there and how places could make people sick.

As I told this story, many of the people were teary eyed. I finished with telling the circle that my spiritual prayers had told me the land was of the Bear Clan and that the spirit of the sleeping Bear had to be wakened for the land to be used for ceremony. I pointed to one teenager, saying he had to help me. As it turned out, he was a Bear Clan member which was perfect for the ceremony.

At this juncture, a Lakota man who was visiting says to me. "Your story is my story. My people have had a Holocaust as well." He began to cry and then told his personal story. Then a Dine' (Navajo) man began, "Your story is my story" and he told his story. After four hours of storytelling, Tom stopped the circle and said, "It's time for lunch."

After lunch, the youth helped the elderly so that all could go to the ceremony site. This is the native way to show respect and care for the elders. As we gathered, I began to call in the spirit with a song I sang in Hebrew; a hawk landed in the middle of the circle and stayed there during the entire ceremony. Then the teenaged boy I had asked to help with the ceremony came with me to look for the proper site where we would awaken the Bear. As we wandered on the land, we found Bear mound unknown to the tribe. Here we spread tobacco and I again sang a song in Hebrew to the Bear spirit asking it to wake up and restore the land in a sacred way.

When we returned, the hawk flew away, and Tom says to me, "I didn't know you know Ho Chunk. That song you sang was a Ho Chunk song." He began to sing it and it did sound similar. Then the Dine' elder said, "I thought you were singing in Dine." And he began to sing the song in Dine'. At this moment, an elderly Ho Chunk woman who was suffering from extreme dementia stood up and says with marked lucidity, "I am not of the Bear Clan, but when I was a little girl, I remembered hearing the Bear clan songs." She began to sing the song from long ago. I told the teenage Bear Clan boy to learn this song that he did not yet know. As soon as he knew the song fully, she sat down and returned to being fully confused.

In the weeks that followed, the tribe was able to hold a number of ceremonies with the youth and restore some links with ancestors, even the Bear ancestor of the place. No one had tended to the spirits of this land for a long time: The Ho Chunk had been forcibly removed by U.S. troops from this land in the 19th century. The ceremony removed obstacles that had previously sabotaged all earlier attempts to teach the traditional ways to Ho Chunk youth, and in essence, brought the spirit Bear out of its colonization-induced slumber.

4. Master and Slave

I was sitting in a room with 50 African-American adolescents, working on peacemaking with them. Many were members of the Black Gangster Disciples. The school had invited me to do a presentation. They were attempting to create an "alternatives to conflict" program.

The youth know what their problems are and it's important to listen to them. Often, they have lots of ideas about what is needed. Certainly, they bring up many issues that fall in the "social justice" category, but many are personal and spiritual.

When I told them about shamanism, they readily engaged: "How do we find a spirit?" "We need spiritual power". "Our problems are so big that only God could deal with them."

I discussed the process of the shaman's journey and asked the teens to journey collectively on what was needed to bring them healing and peace. Strikingly, many came back with journeys that spoke of the wounds of slavery. "We are not slaves, we don't want to be slaves no more to no one," was a common refrain. One of the journeyers got an image of dancing out the conflict of the slaves. The strongest thread connecting their journeys was that we were to create a ritual to heal the wounds of slavery.

For this ritual, some of us drummed for those who volunteered to dance. I invited the dancers to journey to slave ancestors and let them lead the dance. As the dancing began, it was aggressive and fast. Then, some began to shake as if spirits were taking hold, and a rhythmic chant began to emerge. The dance shifted and became more flowing. Still strong and fierce, it lacked its earlier aggressiveness. I encouraged more of the boys to join the dancers.

Later, the dancers described that they felt as if something had taken them over. They wanted me to tell them what had happened. I could not. I asked them what it would be like if they danced "reputation", "respect", and "revenge" instead of acting them out. I emphasized these words as they are key words in their sense of identity.

During the conversations that followed, a conflict between two boys developed. I asked if we could work out the conflict as a group. They agreed. One of the other boys and I journeyed to the spirit of each boy involved, beginning to dance their dance. As we danced, others were to journey and ask for guidance on what to do to change the dance. After a while, they began to join the dance and change it. Their changes were a change in a movement, a few words, or a whole song - whatever came to them. At the end, we brought the two conflicting boys into the dance and had them take part.

Afterwards, the two boys shared their surprise at how "real" the dance seemed to them. I asked if they were as angry as they were before. Both answered that they were not. Through the dance it appeared that each boy was trying to control and dominate the other. Everyone could understand that they were re-creating the story of the master and the slave with each other. When asked if they wanted to continue perpetuating this history, they both shook their head "no". The shamanic ritual had the healing effect of freeing the boys and their ancestors from legacies of transmitted trauma, bringing peace to all.

5. War Spirit from Father to Son

In the first year of the Syrian conflict, I visited Zaatari refugee camp in northern Jordan. At that time 140,000 refugees were living in tents provided by the United Nations High Commissioner for Refugees. The land was completely desolate and rocky. On this particular day, it was windy and sand stung one's eyes. Across the tundra, you could watch sand devils swirling across the land.

I had spent several days interviewing Syrian families and evaluating the level of trauma being experienced amongst the refugees. In today's world of smartphones and computers, many of them would show me videos they had taken of the violence, or pictures of dead bodies of family members killed by the regime. Many would spontaneously lift their shirts or drop their pants to show me bullet wounds or torture scars.

On this particular day, I walked in the big shoes of a special sort of trauma response team: entertainer clowns who had come to soothe and bring healing laughter to the children and families at the camp. As hundreds gathered around, I noticed one isolated little boy, sucking his thumb, holding himself, in a fetal position, wrapped around the anchor rope of a UNHCR tent. I gently put my hand on his back and tried to get him to play pat-a-cakes with me. I deliberately missed his hands and eventually he began to laugh. He was wearing a t-shirt with professional wrestler John Cena on it and I was struck by the irony of a warrior image on such a vulnerable child. I also noticed some bruises on his body that looked like handprints.

Through this whole time, I didn't have a translator assisting me so we were communicating through the world of play and touch. In a subtle way, a spiritual shift occurred and I was putting parts of his soul back into his little body, while pulling what shamans would call a war spirit out of him. Somehow, he had been on the receiving end of the spiritual manifestation of violence. Immediately after this spontaneous healing, he jumped up and joyfully started playing with other children and the clowns.

I next asked around to find this boy's family. I was taken to a tent where I meet his mother. She told me that his father had been depressed and violent since they left Syria. As the handprints suggested, she admitted he had been hitting her and the little boy. I talked with a UNHCR official who arranged to have the father live separately from the family for the interim, until some sort of help could be provided. I met the father to talk with him about what was happening. He was somber and his affect was quite flat. He admitted that then he thought of all the killing he witnessed that had left so many friends and family dead, he would often fly into rage. There and then, when we meet, he wanted to be left alone. Though my translator resisted, I was able to press on to ask if he felt as if someone else is hitting his wife and son. His response was an immediate "yes". I told him it's the spirit of the war that he has witnessed and asked him if I could remove it. The war spirit was extracted, which I symbolically buried in the sand. I managed to do subtle soul retrieval while acting as if I was putting my hand on his heart as an act of compassion. He reported feeling relaxed.

We talked for a while. I told him that I was working to bring trauma healing to the refugees and help the children to not become a lost generation. I told him that I was worried that so few children were going to school and that so many were barraged by nightmares, anxiety, depression, and basically, not thriving; they were barely surviving, after all. He told me that he understood why he must stay in a different tent from his family and invited me to tea.

As I was aware of the transgenerational transmission of trauma, in this case through this "war spirit" that had violently been projected into and by the father, I could help a little boy and his father with the assistance of UNHCR staff to provide a structure of trauma support services for healing their relationship. While extracting the "war spirit" hopefully would calm the situation, an ongoing process of healing would be needed to prevent future violence and rebuild safety, trust, and caring in their relationship.

Conclusion

In many shamanic cultures, transgenerational trauma is viewed as a form of "ancestral soul loss", transmitted by object intrusion, spirit intrusion, breech of taboo, and/or sorcery. When unhealed, these traumas of the past disconnect us from our roots, our families, and from our own sense of belonging. As Anne Ancelin Schutzenberger shares in her seminal work, The Ancestor Syndrome, we are mere links in a chain of generations. In her view, we may have no choice in having the events and traumas experienced by our ancestors visited upon us in our own lifetime. We can, and do, inherit events from our ancestors.

In the shamanic perspective, ancestors are always looking for peace and reconciliation. To reconcile means to "meet again." And in our meeting again, through our connection with the ancestral spirits, we are given opportunity for complete redemption: to redeem the broken connections and heal the wounding.

Healing transgenerational trauma requires the profound ability of symbolic ritual acts. They help to transform space, to communicate that which is invisible to our normal senses, and to transform worldviews, identities, and relationships. Ritual acts can penetrate what often appears intransient and impenetrable in healing transgenerational trauma. Ritual can overwhelm the defenses and convey complex messages, bringing a new consciousness, without saying a single word.

As the case stories attempt to convey, healing ceremony and rituals can breathe life and hope into a community where there is despair. The rituals often make history visible where it has been secret, hidden, denied, or invisible to our knowing. To transcend and heal our inheritance of generations of trauma, we must first be made conscious of them. By their nature these rituals are transformative. They challenge and change the status quo. Symbolically, they become a rite of passage toward a new vision, a new set of values, and a new structure in community life. And in becoming conscious, we are able to make clear choices and take actions to honor the lessons of the past and move into a new dream for the future generations. In this way, we live the Native axiom, "Heal seven generations back, and connect our actions of today for the seven generations forward".

Bibliography

Duran, Eduardo (2006), *Healing the Soul Wound: Counseling with American Indians and Other Native Peoples*, Teachers College Press, N.Y.

Eshowsky, Myron (1999), *Community Shamanism: Youth, Violence, and Healing*, New Village Journal for Building Sustainable Cultures, pp. 28-32

Eshowsky, Myron (2001), "The Spirit of Place and the Healing of History", *Shamanism Journal*, vol.14, no.2, pp.6-12

Gunn Allen, Paula (1992), *The Sacred Hoop: Recovering the Feminine in American Indian Traditions*, Beacon Press.

Mehl-Madrona, Lewis (1998), *Coyote Medicine: Lessons from Native American Healing*, Simon and Schuster Press, New York.

Morrison, Toni (1987), *Beloved*, N.Y., Alfred A. Knopf.

Schirch, Lisa (2005), *Ritual and Symbol in Peacebuilding*, Kumarian Press, Bloomfield, Ct.

Ancelin Schutzenberger, Anne (2009), *The Ancestor Syndrome: Transgenerational Psychotherapy and the Hidden Links in the Family Tree*, Routledge, New York.

Iona Miller is a clinical hypnotherapist (ACHE) and multimedia artist. She bridges the cultural gap between the arts and life-sciences, serves on the Advisory Boards of Journal of Consciousness Exploration & Research, DNA Decipher Journal, and Scientific God Journal, as well as the Board of Directors of Medigrace, Inc. & Calm Birth; a Miami-based Integral Medicine institute.

Ms. Miller worked at Southern Oregon Hypnotherapy, Asklepia Foundation, Institute for Applied Consciousness Science, the Wisdom Center, Science-Art Research Centre Australia, Life Energies Research Institute, and Center for the Study of Digital Life. She coordinates Media & Wellness in the Operations Division of The Osborne Group (TOG).

Website: http://ionamiller.weebly.com

5

Shamanic Doors to Genealogy: Transgenerational Healing through the Family Tree

Iona Miller

"When I worked in my family tree, I understood the strange communion of the destiny that unites me to my ancestors. I had the strong feeling that it was under the influence of events and problems that were incomplete and unresolved by my parents, my grandparents, and my other ancestors. I had the impression that there is often in the family an impersonal Karma transmitted from parents to children. I always knew that I had to answer questions already asked by my ancestors or I had to conclude or continue on the previously unresolved issues". Carl Jung

The integrative process begins with the first steps of our journey, crossing the threshold" to inner psychic life - the hidden realm of the ancestors. We recapitulate soul's mythic journey in mimesis (drama, ritual) and psychobiology, seeking answers to unanswered questions for ourselves. Genealogy is a threshold experience that automatically activates threshold phenomena, shaking up our family tree and leading deeper toward integration.

Shamanic medicine restores power, harmony and spirit. Your "inner shaman" is a bridge between the physical and spirit world. In shamanic journeys we step outside confining personality to "see" the soul and restore power and harmony. The shaman/therapist model is a gestalt, combining powerful consciousness-altering rituals with depth psychologies. More than a simple mix, the paradigm is that healing arises within.

Jungian Wisdom

Psychogenealogy implies transgenerational integration. It allows us to create images not otherwise accessible to our consciousness. We 'paint' a picture of our extended family, and create the bigger stories we need to nourish and sustain us in modern life. We transmute the legacy for our future generations.

We can actively open doors to a dimension where we can work on our psychophysical roots. Estrangement from our ancestor's points to the modern decay of dialogue, essential to our well-being. Instead of estrangement or entanglement, we suggest archetypal recognition of life-themes – the soul of the life cycle.

Our first experience of the process of transformation recapitulates birth. As prototype of the theme of rebirth it may be activated later as religious or spiritual experiences.

"At mid-life another phase begins. The now overdeveloped ego may become so estranged from its mythical roots in psychic experience that the person begins to feel a need for spiritual wholeness, for a meaning in life. During this period the person counteracts the growing sense of alienation by returning to inner experiences or spiritual and religious sources for support and reintegration (Edinger 1973, pp. 37-71). If he is successful, the result is the emergence of a new, more complete identity called the self. This is the culmination of personal actualization; the process of self-development (called individuation) may continue for the rest of the person's life." (Spotts & Shontz)

When he worked his family tree, Jung said in MDR (1997), that partnership with fate became clear to him. Such a partnership binds us all to our ancestors. He added, "I have always felt that I must answer the questions fate put before my ancestors, or that I must finish things they did not have the time to complete" (p, 283).

Soul's Journey

We react to unconscious parental images, heavily influenced by fantasies and archetypal contents. As we work back through our recent ancestors and our Personal Unconscious into the World Tree of shared ancestry, we may be surprised to find that beyond the medieval era we run into legendary and mythological characters "as if" we descend directly from them.

Modern genealogists don't take such material literally, yet such links provide us entrée to the legendary worlds of the Quest for the Holy Grail and our mythic inheritance. While others may see this as mere fiction, we can view it in Hillman's sense as a "healing fiction" and embrace the notion provisionally.

This allows us a more personal relationship with the depths of the Unconscious and Self archetype. Jung carved a motto on his threshold at his Kusnacht home, Vocatus at que non vocatus deus aderit, that is, "Called or not called, the god will be present." It implies we are entering a sacred space.

Ego is challenged with another way of knowing when we shake up our family tree and find missing parts of ourselves in our ancestors within. Adult orphans, a subject not often addressed, may find particular solace in working their tree, reconnecting with what they thought they had lost in new and deeper ways.

Crossing the Threshold

The threshold can involve change guiding toward a preferred state. Kung healers call the threshold of the beyond kia. It is a trance state that they reach through dance, song, and concentration.

Threshold also refers to phenomena other than tangible matter. For example, a psychic threshold refers to the place of transition from one belief to another or the shift from one state of being to another. Thus threshold is both place and process. As place, it is the point of transition marking the boundary between two opposing regions (Barrie, 1996); as process, threshold holds together the tension inherent in duality and paradox (Eliade, 1987). The entrance, beginning, and opening to a state or action (Onions, 1955), threshold is a powerful place of communication between the opposing worlds that lie on either side of it - the profane temporal world of history, of human affairs and events, on the one side, and the sacred metaphysical world of soul or psyche on the other (Eliade, 1987).

Threshold is the in-between zone where passage from one sphere or one way of being to another is made possible. Inside and outside, sacred and profane, psyche and matter, conscious and unconscious, are among the significant "regions" that the threshold both divides and brings together at its borders. At its essence, threshold is the stable center that mediates between and holds the tension of the opposites; it is a place of possibilities where both sides have the potential to be seen and where energy has the opportunity to flow in either direction. (Buck, 2004)

Traditional wisdom says, "to forget one's ancestors is to be a tree without a root." Combining personal, familial, and collective talents we transform our destiny by analyzing and integrating familial patterns. If we are fortunate, our living elders describe both the factual and imaginal family (legendary ancestors, distorted family stories, self-delusions, and misapprehensions) to us directly. If ritual is a channel to the ancestors, psychogenealogy is such a ritual, literally and metaphorically.

In The Earth Has a Soul, Jung says, "Moreover, my ancestors' souls are sustained by the atmosphere of the house, since I answer for them the questions that their lives once left behind. I carve out rough answers as best I can. I have even drawn them on the walls. It is as if a silent, greater family, stretching down the centuries, were peopling the house."

Genealogy is a mythic journey. The threshold is an archetype of beginnings, the initial conditions of the unfolding fractal of our psychic process. The threshold challenges us to follow the call of our ancestors and begin our quest for deeper meaning. It may be more of a crisis, a birth or death in the family that spurs the process. Our threshold moments may be full of anxiety or tentative ambivalence.

Transgenerational Integration means risking transgenerational wounding and healing. Sometimes there are obstacles and ordeals. Some of our family lines will lead to Dead Ends or impenetrable Brick Walls. Other lines simply go extinct. Life's thresholds include the grief of death, the anxiety of birth, and the trepidation of the unknown. Family is the initiatory vessel in which our raw psyche is alchemically cooked and transformed. We reclaim what has been lost.

As in shamanic training, we begin our epic journey when we cross the first threshold. Initially, we don't need to be concerned with the therapeutic issues. Healings are natural consequences of the unfolding process. You don't have to try to get into a state. The process will carry you through creative research and work on life-issues, genealogical challenges, and process.

Our initial meeting with our ancestors may be the most meaningful. We may encounter our core issues right away in our closest relatives – the family shadow. There will be tragedy and trauma in your family tree – beyond shock, shame, and blame. We may be poised to pass such traumas down through our offspring, through epigenetics or toxic behaviors.

Likewise, psychogenealogy can be healing, uncovering and resolving old secrets or mysteries. Crossing the return threshold involves sharing what we have found with the family and perhaps the world. We may find new creative ways to do so and live from and with that knowledge. What are you preserving? What haunts you? What family secrets have you found, kept, or shared; which have found you?

Loss of ancestors can be likened to loss of soul. Soul-knowing includes who we are and where we come from. This is the foundation upon which the threshold is built. Such knowledge is otherwise inaccessible to ordinary ego consciousness. Crossing the threshold can be serious business, best approached with reverence. The grave can also be a threshold as a point of passage.

Combining personal, familial, and collective talents can transform our destiny by analyzing and integrating familial patterns.

Like a dream, this remembrance is a jumping off point for further self-exploration. While working the fractal nature of the family system, we insist on the particularity or specificity of any individual's life story and the singularity of historical situations.

Genealogy can be approached as a curatorial project – collecting, ordering and honoring. Ritual grounds us and manifests spiritual potential. It connects us to the wisdom of the ancients and the subconscious mind. Through remembrance and conscious awareness of our ancestors, we give them our attention, contemplation, and compassion.

Such techniques are thresholds that act as Doors to the Dead, which shamanic societies have always found powerful. Our ancestors are a natural part of the universal mindfield and the personal mindfield we embody. Epigenetics supports this view that inheritable non-physical changes in DNA expression -- turning genes on and off -- can change the whole system. If a single trauma can create a wound, a healing moment can transform it.

Describing the heroic journey, Joseph Campbell describes 'crossing of the threshold' as an initiatory act that leads beyond the commonplace into the collective unconscious. But we don't just cross it once; we cross it over and over again, each time pushing the limits of our previous findings. We discover signs, synchronicities, fingers pointing at the moon.

We leave our known limits and venture off into the unknown. Psychogenealogy provides an unfolding narrative for just such a soul journey. It is the beginning of our own particular way - a genealogical conversion of all lineage threads - back to the origin of all creation, the original common genetic ancestors.

Sheelahs

The significance of the threshold can be precise or ambiguous, a moment or a process. We can presume the first thresholds – dark thresholds -- were the mouths of labyrinthine caves, which echo our expulsion from the confines of the womb, and any birth trauma associated with it, as well described by Grof's perinatal states.

In the Druid tradition, or native folk religion, the Sheela-na-Gig symbolically represent our primordial origin, our genealogical and genetic ground zero – the feminine essence of creation exposing her naked genitals.

Sheelahs are often associated with doors, or Thresholds in the British Isles. Their significance is directly related to earlier Goddess/Fertility figures and the Goddess symbolism of the early pre-historic and Celtic periods. Sheelahs appeared during the latter part of the Celtic Christian period through the later Middle Ages. No two alike, some may be older relics re-set into medieval buildings.

Sheelas are found in liminal or borderline positions, above doorways, by windows, or gables. There is one built into the wall of the Nunnery on the sacred island of Iona in Scotland. As female deities or Goddesses, they were placed on churches, castles and other important buildings from the medieval period until quite recently.

They acted as dedicatory or protective symbols promoting good luck and fertility. Some of these entrance shrines have touch-holes, the traces of girdles and the signs of objects descending from the genital area or lying between the legs of the figure. Some say the sheelas were to arrest the Evil Eye (Freitag).

They were erected over the doorways of churches and castles and overlooking holy wells or gate pillars. This suggests that they were a very potent and powerful image with a deeper communal value, perhaps melding the new Christian and old folkways. Sheela-na-Gigs may have evolved from the Goddess symbolism of the Neolithic, Bronze Age, and Celtic periods. Passing through such an aperture recapitulates birth with rebirth. It is also a primal encounter with the Dweller on the Threshold, between the conscious and the unconscious.

Neumann (1972) saw the feminine archetype in "the house, door, threshold, and tomb." His three most important and eternal threshold experiences are the processes of birth, maturation, and death. In ancient China both newborn infants and the dying were placed upon the ground. Eliade says, "To be born or to die, to enter the living family or the ancestral family (and to leave one or the other), there is a common threshold, one's native Earth."

The Earth herself decides if the birth or death is valid. The true Mother legitimizes and confers protection. Sometimes the sick are buried for regeneration and rebirth. Initiation requires a ritual death and resurrection. We recognize double movement: when something is created or comes into life, we should give some offering back to the Divine Darkness recognizing the authorization for something to live even for a limited time. Devoting time and attention to psychogenealogy can be one such offering.

Movement toward self-integration and transgenerational integration is another threshold. Eliade (1987) describes the shamanic roots of threshold symbolism. It represents not only the difference between two spaces but also between two ways of being, and a vehicle of passage. Eliade says, "The threshold is the limit, the boundary, the frontier that distinguishes and opposes two worlds – and at the same time the paradoxical place where those worlds communicate where passage from the profane to the sacred world becomes possible."

This ritual function extends to thresholds in human habitations and houses of the dead. In the ancient Middle East, the threshold was a judgment place. Sacrifices or libations to guardian divinities or demons are offered here. Within the sacred precinct the profane is transcended. Communication with the depths becomes possible.

The point of reference remains the threshold experience, which we can associate with our psychogenealogical journey, where we go from ordinary awareness toward the synchronous and numinous. M.-L. von Franz ratifies this notion:

"Synchronistic events are therefore characterized by the intrusion into our "normal" state of consciousness a second psychic state, which usually remains below the threshold. In our normal state of consciousness we are seldom aware of the fact that the unconscious psyche makes a substantial contribution to our perception of reality and that we can never perceive reality as such...."

Doors to the Dead

This is the work of the soul. Genealogy functions as a map of the psyche -- a map to the archaic threshold through which the ancestors await us. While we go through many doors, the crossing of the first liminal threshold is special. Crossing the Return Threshold is the full-circle completion of our quest – the search for self.

Dividing inner and outer inhabited space, doorways signify transition and transformation. While the term 'portal' has become a New Age buzzword for all sorts of nonsense, out of the hands of the fabulists it remains a profound psychic reality that can initiate our spiritual journey. We can enter the transgenerational story of ourselves through genealogy with a sense of reverence for sacred space and mystery.

The door to our ancestral past holds the key to our own myth of origin -- the vast migrations and epic challenges faced by those who brought us to the eternal present. Through them we are temporarily immortal. Our whole psychophysical being, both structural and ephemeral, is our memory -- personal and collective. We are informed by their presence as well as their genes. They may venture forth from the portal of sleep in our dreams.

Be the Key; Open Me

Doors or gates often have guardians. Imagine you are the guardian of the labyrinth of your ancestral lines and those of your future generations. What would you do to nurture, sustain, and protect them? What intuitive and creative methods can you employ?

Opening the door in your tree itself serves as an 'entrance meditation,' the first part of the inner journey. We may feel we are answering a deeper calling to decode the chronicle of our significance. We may find exemplar characters that embody guides, the shadow, anima/animus and our higher selves.

What family secrets might you find behind the door? How we are like them is as important as how we differ, or how we wish we were different. When we confront their stories we know such things immediately. We discover that others have been there before us when the door to the World Tree of shared ancestry swings wide. There may be impressions, apprehensions, or symbols that gradually reveal themselves to our conscious minds.

This frees us from trying to deal with our issues on the apparent level of things, without any depth and meaning, apart from any dialogue with life. It opens the perspectives, a relief from most everyday discourses in our lives. You may think that you are living "here and now", but chances are that you are unconsciously reenacting unresolved issues of your ancestors. The need to address our genealogy reflects a general law of life for how we want to become ourselves. There is significant evidence that these ancient schema 'haunt' the present, waiting for conscious integration.

'Doors to the dead' appear as freestanding portals, dolmans, causewayed ring-ditches, stone henges, or thresholds to grave mounds or cave shrines. The passage tomb at Newgrange has a sculpted entrance stone. Archaeologists in Transylvania discovered a "tepes", cave/mine or rath with a fire-pit dating to 5000 BCE.

On the ancient Isle of Iona, the dead or volunteer sacrifices were buried in the doorway to prevent the walls from caving in -- another offering to the Dark Divine in return for existential support. Many believe Relig Odhráin has been in continuous use as a royal graveyard since St. Columba's day, 500 CE. It became the traditional burial place for the Kings of Dalriada and Scotland for many centuries. Macbeth lies there, plus 48 Scottish kings, 8 Norwegian and 4 Irish rulers.

Sacred doorways connect the dead and the living, as controllable boundaries forming between-spaces. Such deviant spaces summoned the supernatural to obtain contact with the dead in the Otherworld, materially and metaphorically. In Iona, the veil between worlds is traditionally considered 'thin,' encouraging 'second sight.' Jung said second sight is a 'gift' that carried the burden of responsibility. Perhaps we should call such vision 'first sight' as it is more primordial.

Liminal Lineage

Your own genealogy and the pursuit of your lineage and name provide a metaphorical door to connect with and approach the dead. This key to the labyrinth of self-knowledge holds answers to the perennial question, "Who am I?" Where we come from is related to where we are going. As Gaillard (2020) shows, this quest and the renascence that emerges through it is the real message of Sophocles in this masterpiece on Oedipus.

Genealogy is a highly ritualized environment, with rites of contemplative or meditative research, entry work, synchronicities, documentation, initiations to genealogical or bloodline groups, and pilgrimage. This is a metaphor we live by that can expand our sense of self-knowledge. Each time we learn about an ancestor we knock on a door. Knowledge is the key that unlocks the door, the direct experience of gnosis. Our attention enlivens their presence.

The door controls access and marks the boundary between antagonistic and confrontational spaces or a psychophysical transition in social roles. This architectural element allows us to abandon one space for the next. Doors and thresholds are thus closely linked with rites of passage. Not every crossing of a threshold is a liminal ritual but the opportunity with many social and metaphorical implications is there.

The Soul Foretells

Like remembering the past, consciousness of the future depends on where you get your information in an intuitive leap. If we 'go to the future' we can "see" in our contemplation what is going on if we visualize the problem. As described by physicist Fred Alan Wolf and others, the future is already there, 'around the corner.' Certain potential pathways are more accessible than others, following the path of least resistance, unless you modify your path of least action.

Relaxing into a self-aware state of that future time, you intentionally drift off into a twilight state. There is no need to force it. You can potentially 'undo' things in the past and create new potential for the future. It matters little whether such experiences, shamanic journeys or vision quests, are 'real' or imaginal. The effects are real and change our attitudes, which change our being.

The Mindfield

We don't have to take it literally, nor dismiss it. If we don't sense it, it isn't there. We have to make a move in that direction. It is already out there for us to experience, certainly in terms of healing and transformation. Faith and trust in our ability to be on the right track increases creativity.

The same is true moving through your genealogical lines. How would you describe your relationship with your grandmother, with your ancestral women? Have you ever had a vision of a female wisdom figure? How do the men in your pedigree differ from the men of today? How might our ancestors have affected our relational and spousal choices?

Much of genealogical and psychogenealogical best-practice includes mythic and fictional characters. So, the process is best approached with a Jungian orientation, rather than as hard historical fact. It has psychic reality, and Jungian and post-Jungian practices allow us to interact poetically with such material in a deeply meaningful way that enhances personal and transgenerational integration.

The Taking In of Solace: The Many Into One

The Portuguese word "Saudade" describes the feeling of intensively missing something -- a yearning for the future or connection to a destiny in time that is NOT YET. It may be a particular skill or gift of the genetic serpent inhabiting time itself. It transcends us all.

This melancholic longing is for an absent beloved who might never return, such as a lost lover, or a missing family member, or one unborn or who failed to thrive, moved away, separated, or died.

Saudade is "the love that remains" after someone is gone. Emptiness is an integral aspect of mind/matter and psychophysical being. This emotional vacuum can be likened to the Void or absolute vacuum of space which is actually a plenum of infinite potential. Sad and happy feelings come all together.

Self-Initiation

Hillman said, "the community of the dead .... are already there, like presences waiting for you." Like the ancient Egyptians, we can 'open the mouth of the dead.' You can reunite through genealogical practice without dying. Ritual initiation requires a formal symbolic ego-death and rebirth but this occurs as a natural effect of engagement with our depths.

Jung said transpersonal psychic life "is the mind of our ancient ancestors, the way in which they thought and felt, the way in which they conceived of life and the world, of gods and humans beings. The existence of these historical layers is presumably the source of belief in reincarnation and in memories of past lives," (Jung, 1939, p.24).

In 'Extending the Family' (1985), Hillman says, "With the passing of time a sense of its power grows within one's psyche, like the movements of its skeleton inside one's flesh, which keeps one in servitude to patterns entombed in our closest attitudes and habits. From this interior family we are never free. This service keeps us bonded to the ancestors." Some report a sort of "calling illness" until they respond to the ancestors calling them to do the life-enhancing work.

He also suggests we "turn the trap of entanglement in the personal family into an archetypal recognition of family as the supreme metaphor for sustaining the human condition," (pg. 6). In this sense, our genealogical work signifies a Homecoming, like that of Odysseus, it extends beyond meaningful connections of the nuclear family into our vast archetypal family with its full imagistic panoply.

Such family therapy isn't restricted to standard theories and practices but to the epistemology that informs them. It is not an investigation of historical causality, but a circular, synchronistic, non-linear epistemology with archetypal considerations. The influence is interactional with the positive teleological functions of the symptoms. Within the pedigree we encounter representations of the actual forces of epoch-making political, economic, philo-sophical, and religious collectives.

A 2011 study in the European Journal of Social Psychology suggests that thinking about one's genetic origin (i.e. ancestors) provides us with a positive psychological resource that increases their intellectual performance. They tested this by manipulating whether participants thought about their ancestors or not (manip-ulation of ancestor salience). Then, they measured their expected and actual intellectual performance in a variety of intelligence tasks.

"Four studies supported our assumptions: participants show higher expected (Study 1) and actual intellectual performance (Studies 2–4) when they are reminded about their ancestors. We also have initial evidence that this effect may be fueled by in-creased levels of perceived control and promotion orientation" (Fischer, et al).

Psychogenealogy is a process of self-initiation – a vital part of the Great Work, much like alchemy or meditation. Initiation simply means "beginning," a dedication to a sacred practice. Once you get the ball rolling, it rolls of its own momentum. You make the first gesture, an explicit commitment to realize your potential within the method. The meaning of this commitment unfolds slowly over a lifetime.

The World Tree contains ample opportunities for both self-realization and the experience of chaos, multiplicity, and disin-tegration. In this sense, psychogenealogy reflects the nature of the soul: 1) makes all meanings possible, 2) turns events into ex-periences, 3) involves a deepening of experiences, 4) is communicated in love, 5) and has a special relation with death, (Hillman, 1977, p. xvi, Hillman, 1976, pp. 44-47).

We can apply much of what we learn in this process. The recollection of feelings, experiences, places or pleasurable events and well-being stimulates the senses and guides us toward living into our psychophysical potential. Tangible, symbolic, and imaginal experience of our ancestors and progeny can have real effects on our attitudes and compassion. The effect is Transgenerational Integration. By embracing the World Tree we find transgenerational healing.

References

Buck Stephanie, (2004), *Home, Hearth, and Grave: The Archetypal Symbol of Threshold On the Road to Self*, http://jungiansociety.org/index.php/home-hearth-and-grave-the-archetypal-symbol-of-threshold-on-the-road-to-self

Edinger Edward, (1973), *Ego and Archetype*, Shambhala.

Eliade Mircea, (1987), *The Sacred and the Profane*, Harcourt Brace Jovanovich.

Fischer Peter, Anne Sauer, Claudia Vogrincic, and Silke Weisweiler, (2011), *The ancestor effect: Thinking about our genetic origin enhances intellectual performance*, European Journal of Social Psychology, Volume 41, Issue 1, pages 11–16, Feb. 2011.

Freitag Barbara, (2004), *Sheelah-na-Gigs: Unravelling an Enigma*, Routledge, New York, NY.

Gaillard T. Tony, (2020), *Transgenerational Healing of Oedipus at Colonus*, Genesis Editions, Geneva.

Grof Stanislaw, (1988), *The Adventure of Self Discovery*, State Univ of New York Pr.

Hillman J. (1976). *Suicide and the Soul*. New York: Harper Colophon.

Hillman J. (1977), *Re-Visioning Psychology*. New York: Harper Perrenial.

Hillman James (1985), *Extending the Family: From Entanglement to Embrace*, The Texas Humanist 7/4, (1985): 6-11.

Hillman James, (1998), *Healing Fiction*, Spring Publications.

Jung C.G. (1989), *Memories, Dreams, Reflections*, Vintage.

Jung C.G., (2002), *The Earth Has a Soul: C.G. Jung on Nature, Technology & Modern Life*, Meredith Sabini (Editor), Joseph Henderson M.D., North Atlantic Books; 1 edition (May 28, 2002).

Miller Iona (2015), *Sacred Wounding: The Family Shadow - Transgenerational Wounding & Healing*, http://jungiangenealogy.weebly.com/sacred-wounding.html

Miller Iona (2014), *Jungian Genealogy: Bridge of the Spirits* http://jungiangenealogy.weebly.com/sacred-wounding.html

Miller Iona (2015), *Ancestors & Archetypes*, http://ancestorsandarchetypes.weebly.com/

Neumann Erich, (1972), *The Great Mother*, Princeton University Press.

Spotts James and Shontz Franklin, (1980), "Life-Theme Theory of Chronic Drug Abuse", in *Theories on Drug Abuse*, NIDA Research Monograph 30, March 1980, Ed. Dan J. Lettierr, et al.

Von Franz M.-L., (1985), *Projection and Re-Collection in Jungian Psychology, Reflections of the Soul*, p. 195, Open Court Publishing Company.

Tony Thierry Gaillard is a Swiss psychotherapist and re-searcher, specializing in psychoanalysis, transgenerational integration and psychogenetics. He graduated at the University of Geneva and at the City University of New York in Developmental Psychology (M.A.). Then he trained in psychoanalysis, philosophy and explored multiple therapeutic approaches. He practices in private since 1998.

In four recent books (see bibliography), he proposes a new thesis on the Oedipus myth that leads to a new psychological paradigm to reharmonize our relationship to the world.

His website: www.en.t-gaillard.com

6

Sophocles, Psycho-shamanic Ancestor

Tony T. Gaillard

The shamanic perspective of healing and restoration of harmony also concerns the two millennia conflict between traditional societies and the so-called modern society. It is in Athens that the conflict began with the emergence of our civilization, nearly five centuries BC. Restoring the balance between tradition and modernity, this is exactly the purpose of Sophocles, the famous Athenian dramatist, priest of the healer god Asclepius. With his work on Œdipus, Sophocles has left a cathartic healing model, illustrating the transformation of the chaos arising from the conflict between ancient knowledge and new knowledge, towards restoring harmony and prosperity.

As we will see, Œdipus' initiation to self-knowledge, to know the gods and the universe looks like those of the shamans in traditional societies. After going through the worst trials, becoming the hero of Colonus and ensuring prosperity, Œdipus is like these shamans who take care of their community. But the peculiarity of Sophocles is that he had to adapt ancestral wisdom to this new situation with the birth of our civilization, which spawned a new type of conflict that now opposes traditional and modern values. Because he takes into account both the ancient traditions as the change of civilization (like it or not), and the new world that is emerging, Sophocles embodies a new kind of shaman, a psycho-shaman.

In this article, I will present the main lines of the model that Sophocles has left us to transcend a conflict whose consequences - environmental, human, and spiritual - are now the headlines. Pioneering and misunderstood so far, Sophocles' teaching is a model of harmonizing the relationship between tradition and modernity.

The historic turning point in Athens

From Egypt and other distant lands, many spiritual and shamanic traditions converged on this new Promised Land that was Greece in antiquity, the cradle of arts, democracy, philosophy and science. Until the 5th century BC, shamanism had evolved by adapting to its time, producing a trail of healers (disciples of Asclepius in Epidaurus), mediums (the Pythia of Delphi), masters (Pythagoras) and other visionaries so as to create favorable conditions for the emergence of new forms of knowledge., Alchemy gave birth to a new form of civilization In the cauldron of Athens, more rational and so-called modern and democratic, with the beginnings of scientific medicine (Hippocrates), physics (Thales, Archimedes) and metaphysical philosophy.

But who would have thought that this new knowledge would denigrate and oppose itself to the traditions? Who could have predicted that the newly created being would turn against the hand that fed him? And yet that is what happens in Athens, during this historic turning point that saw the birth of our civilization. Like a tidal wave, this new civilization imposes its own representation of reality that plunges the ancient traditions into the dark, until they get forgotten. The word "mythology" is invented to denigrate the old beliefs which from now on rely only on reason alone, without any reference to the irrational. Rites of passage, the occult, poetry and everything related to non-rational dimensions pass for childish because they are neither understood nor perceived. "Those that were seen dancing were taken for fools by those who did not hear the music," says Nietzsche. Like him, savvy intellectuals have always denounced the drift of the collective consciousness, ever more limited. That is why Nietzsche considers the change of civilization as a step backwards and not as progress, "God is dead, and it is we who have killed him!"

The scars of this ancient failed marriage between traditional cultures and modern ones are still visible around us within ourselves. This story will continue to haunt the present as long as it remains incomplete and not integrated. We project this heritage to the outside world, fueling conflicts instead of really solving them, because it is usually unconscious. But the integration of old unresolved conflicts is part of the harmonization work and the restoration of peace with our ancestors, things that shamans, and many other initiates, have always sought to do. But the arrival of a new civilization, ours, poses a new problem to ancestral practices.

To continue fulfilling their spiritual and healing functions, the old practices cannot ignore these changes and their impact on the collective consciousness. The core-shamanism, neo-shamanism, or psycho-shamanism, reflects the recognition of the true psychological, social and cultural life of today. As C. Michael

Smith[1] explains, what good would it be to participate in ceremonies and other traditional shamanic initiations if their benefits are not reflected in our daily lives? To recover what was forgotten or repressed, with the arrival of our modern civilization, more work is needed. For example we can learn to communicate with the symbolic and subconscious world, with the "language of birds" in the words of the psychoanalyst Erich Fromm (*The Forgotten Language: An Introduction to the Understanding of Dreams, Fairy Tales and Myths*, E. Fromm) and reconnect with our inner being[2]. As witness to the change of civilization, both heir of tradition and avant-garde tragedian with his works of "tragic" vision, Sophocles enables us to articulate the change in civilization without denying ancestral wisdom, nor excluding ourselves from the world ahead. With the story of the healing of Œdipus, Sophocles has left us a teaching that transcends the division between traditional consciousness and that consciousness which characterizes our culture today.

Since time immemorial, mythology has provided access to the symbolic world, timeless and unconscious, where the unresolved conflicts in history still belong. With myths, all sorts of problems and themes can be made conscious, discussed, and eventually integrated into higher order. Sometimes it is necessary to rewrite the myths to meet new needs and new situations. Those who rewrite them, like Sophocles, lend essential support to the work of

---

[1] See C. Michael Smith's interview published in this book.
[2] Let's also note that there are also movements of modernity going to ancestral wisdom, such as phenomenology in philosophy, Binswanger's Daseinanalysis, Carl Jung with its references to the "numinous", and more recently, the whole movement called "transgenerational".

collective integration and thus the maintenance of harmony. Since the first shamanic societies have not been confronted with the conflicts generated by the birth of a new civilization, a new challenge awaits ancient traditions. This is precisely what will occupy Sophocles. Like many of his contemporaries, he was well aware of the problems caused by this opposition between old traditions and new civilization being born before his eyes. And the epidemic of plague that ravaged Athens was for him, as for all those attentive to the hidden meaning of events, the sign of a profound imbalance that it was crucial to recover.

Although he would not live long enough to expect to see the situation recover in Athens, Sophocles felt the need to leave to posterity a new healing model that is extremely important today. With reference to the consequences of the conflict between civilizations, he began his work on Œdipus with the description of the ravages of the plague. It is a metaphor that refers to the amount of pain from a disruption of forces: epidemics, environmental disasters, unconscious leaders, etc.

The rejection of tradition

With the development of the new civilization of reason, the iconoclastic, the unconscious, the symbolic, the sacred and the spiritual are devalued and repressed. In Athens, what was so important to their ancestors became whims in the eyes of an unwise but assertive community, the strong majority in a democratic system. To the laws of "natural" life, followed by their ancestors, men now preferred to write and enforce their own laws according to their own criteria. This history that began in Athens has continued to repeat itself. It replayed itself in the colonization movements, for example, in South and North America and around the world. The sons of the earth are replaced by the citizens, sons of the city and its laws, or children in the institutions, meeting these new laws written by men, often in total disagreement with the laws of life and of nature. And it's always the same story that we see repeat in Greenland, Tibet, Indonesia, Africa, the Amazon, etc.

History repeats this opposition between tradition and modernity along the lines of what happened in Athens. It is this tendency to promote new beliefs on the back of old (misunderstood) beliefs which continues to feed the duality. That is why the sages have withdrawn from the political scenery: to report the truth is neither salesworthy nor a matter of proselytizing or beliefs.

From Matriarchy to Modernity

If we want to take into account the source of a good number of problems that we have today, we are brought back to what happened in Athens at the beginning of civilization change. Let's briefly recall that this transition from a traditional to the so-called modern civilization is itself the consequence of a deeper change: the famous passage from matriarchy to modernity. Unilaterally matriarchal societies became radically modern, in an extreme reversal movement, difficult to balance. This reversal follows the awareness of the role of man and of sexuality in procreation. As long as our ancestors believed that women were creating children alone, they imposed a totalitarian regime of fusion and undifferentiating which prohibited emancipation.

As the concept of father did not exist, it was as if "dead" or non-existent in the matriarchal mind. The limits of the matriarchal consciousness is found in its ignorance of the edification function of the father, of his Word which would likely bring forth the true subject (or true self) extracting him from the procreative womb. Pressing against this limit; the forces of emancipation will cause a reverse reaction, or counter-culture, which will instead promote the art of thinking (philosophy), the spirit of research, the development of science. If it is a source of creativity, this tension between the two regimes threatens to produce profound imbalances.

The test of reality (the resemblance between father and son) highlights the denial of the father and provides arguments for reducing the womb to the role of female receptacle of the male seed of life. This change of perspective was passionately debated in antiquity. In particular, it changed the balance of power among the gods. They say Athena, the protector of Athens, emerged from the head of Zeus, without needing a mother[3]...

The birth of our modern civilization coincides with the shift from matriarchal to patriarchal regimes. And when it grows too unilaterally, modernity also produces its own set of symptoms. In turning against the old matriarchal traditions, this new modern regime cuts us off from the sources, from the mother, who becomes a forbidden love (now accused of incest). From the *mythos* to the *logos*, the language becomes repressive, pseudo-educational. The iconoclasm and metaphysics of modernity lose the relationship with being, with this oceanic feeling of being in contact with or in the presence of the greater whole, or with the Great

---

[3] This can be seen as the metaphorically similar situation that is now taking place with medical tools replacing natural procreation (where the medical system is representative of the father and its rational worldview), or the power of money (also a biases for the human to substitute natural laws) with the hiring of surrogate mothers.

Spirit as the Indians of North America would say. Certainly we must emancipate from the omnipotence and alienating fusion of the womb, but without being cut off from our roots or losing the link to ancestors. As we will see, with his model of transgenerational integration, Sophocles has the solution.

In his work on Œdipus, Sophocles meets all these lineage issues, with respect to ancestors and origins. These themes are omnipresent in his mind, sometimes explicitly, sometimes implicitly. For example, Œdipus is a victim of adoptive parents who hide his true origins. This situation leads to the tragedy told in King Œdipus. Here the message is clear: to deprive a person of the truth about the identity of his parents is to set up future tragedies. Instead of talking about their infertility, Polybius and Merope decide to evade their problem and to hide his adoption from Œdipus. Somehow, in the etymological sense, they make a pact with the devil, in reference to the Latin *diabolo*, where "dia" means to separate, "he who divides" the word from what it should relate to (as opposed to the reunification word function of the symbols). If traditional societies were aware of the transgenerational laws and respected them, this knowledge was lost with the development of our civilization. Today, those who pervert the relationship to the truth, especially regarding lineage, seem to ignore the consequences. If they were aware of transgenerational laws, they would soon restore the truth and free themselves from their own alienation.

The case of Œdipus illustrates how the secrecy surrounding his origins engenders the miseries that plague him and Thebes the city that placed him on his throne. This is the symptom caused by a modern culture which hat cut off the link to being and to Mother Earth, and which has lost the awareness of the dramatic consequences of such secrecy. An ignorance that characterizes our society today, ignorant of the laws of nature, flouts them without even realizing it. If traditionally the individual existed only in connection with a family and / or place of origin, depriving these links and these roots does not bring anything good (although modern society claims to promote individualization). This loss of consciousness and the transgression of old laws generates new tragedies as Sophocles demonstrates with the arrival of the plague in Thebes. But already in these times, few people would understand the real causes of these disasters, or they would withdraw from public life. Today, with transgenerational analysis we rediscover the relevance of this ancient knowledge.

Because he knows the transgenerational laws, Sophocles' approach is therapeutic. With his work on Œdipus, Sophocles exposes an alternative to fusion (matriarchal) or cutting (modern). This alternative is to integrate the origins, the lineage and the links to ancestors while emancipating from alienating links. Sophocles shows that it is by becoming subjectively oneself that we emancipate without being cut from the world and from the being, a process that integrates the ancient rites of passage from childhood to adulthood. In his testamentary work, *Œdipus at Colonus*, Sophocles shows the transformation of Œdipus which he associates with the healing of the plague. Finally, Œdipus becomes the hero of Colonus, guarantor of prosperity, completing the transformation of the plague that was raging at the beginning of the story. Thus, even for the worst situation, Sophocles leaves a healing model that transcends the opposition between tradition and modernity to restore harmony.

Who was Sophocles?

At the time of Sophocles, the inspired poets, authors of tragic plays, had the function of being the guides of the collective consciousness. In huge amphitheaters, they addressed their messages to the greatest number and dealt with events that were calling the whole community. With these new collective rituals, they provided answers to complex situations by drawing on some old traditions, as well as new provocative ideas.

As a dramatist, Sophocles belong to the continuation of shamanic work, for the welfare of the community, to restore the balance when the situation requires it, as when his city was ravaged by the plague. Indeed, from 430-426 BC, several epidemic waves ravaged Athens. A third of the population did die of the infection that nobody knew how to heal. The situation was catastrophic; even sacred places were strewn with unburied corpses. Helpless facing the violence of the scourge, the Athenians had lost all respect for the divine. Customs hitherto effective for burials were disrupted. They buried the bodies right away and left, without having time to follow the traditional rituals, sometimes throwing one on top of another...

In the capital totally adrift, restoring harmony is a huge challenge for Sophocles, to the measure of his genius. Alongside his work as author of tragic plays, Sophocles assumed many functions, administrator, a general but also a more traditional and religious role as a priest of the god Asclepius the healer. He had the great honor to harbor the statue of the god in his own house, while the dedicated temple was under construction. As a dramatist, Sophocles won the largest annual competition twenty-four times, placing second the other times. From his many works, over a hundred according to estimates, only seven remain. Among these, there is the famous story of Antigone and the two plays dedicated to Œdipus, *Œdipus the King*, and *Œdipus at Colonus*, which will be his last play, his testament. At age eighty-three he was still an elected member of the ten advisers to restore order to a city in crisis. Though progressive, a democrat well informed of the progress of reason, Ionian physics, and the writings of Hippocrates, unlike others Sophocles did not withdraw from ancient traditions. He died in 406 BC, two years before the historic defeat of Athens (404 BC), after twenty-seven years of wars against the Spartans.

Summary of Sophocles' Œdipus myth (in two parts)

Œdipus King (or Œdipus-Rex)

To save Thebes from a terrible plague, the king Œdipus consults the seer Tiresias. The latter explains that they must clarify the circumstances of the murder of the precedent King, Laius. Œdipus promises to punish the guilty and begins an investigation that will lead him to discover himself. Gradually, the information overlaps and Œdipus discover that he has been secretly adopted by those he took for his parents, Polybius and Merope. At birth, he was abandoned to the wild beasts of Mount Cithaeron for him to die there. However, a shepherd of the neighboring kingdom saved him from certain death. Then Œdipus learns that the stranger who had attacked him a long time ago, and he had killed, was Laius, his own father ! And the queen who was given to him with the throne, as a reward for having defeated the Sphinx that terrorized Thebes, is none other than his own mother, Jocasta, the former wife of Laius!

When the truth comes out, Jocasta hangs herself and Œdipus, mad with despair, blinds himself, since all appearances were obviously false.

Œdipus at Colonus

After a long restless wandering on the roads accompanied by his daughter Antigone, Œdipus arrives at Colonus, a small town close to the capital Athens. Theseus, king of the region, is the first man to finally give them hospitality and protection. This return of Œdipus into the community is due to Theseus' noble heart. He sees Œdipus clearly, beyond his terrible reputation. Œdipus has gone through the worst trials; it is now another man who attracts the favor of the gods. "It's when I'm nothing that I become a man," he explains to his daughter. Finally, the gods call him to leave this world. To Theseus, worthy of his love, Œdipus bequeaths a secret that will ensure the prosperity of his kingdom. But in order that this prosperity would last forever Œdipus should not be forgotten (i.e. ancestor cult).

At the beginning of the first play, *King Œdipus*, Sophocles describes the situation he has seen with his own eyes in his city of Athens. The plague sterilized all sources of life, humans, animals and the vegetal world. And at the end, it is the guarantee of prosperity that ends the second play, *Œdipus at Colonus*. Understanding the teaching of Sophocles means having discovered how to go from worst to best. We have to decipher this teaching between the lines of his text because, of course, this kind of knowledge is not passed on as it is done today in universities - in an essentially intellectual form. As in the initiatory tradition, Sophocles hides his teaching, not arbitrarily, but because his message calls for an opening of the mind and the ability to go beyond appearances to discover truths inaccessible at first.

Sophocles' method consists in letting us believe Œdipus deserves the tragic fate that punctuates the end of the first piece. In doing so he goes in the direction of modern thinking. But this is not its true purpose, quite the contrary. While one might think Œdipus deserved his punishment, in order to raise the audience's awareness to another level (to another state of consciousness), Sophocles creates a surprise effect with different denouement, the heroic ending at Colonus. He invites us to go beyond the level of a first reading level to follow the course of what now looks like an initiation. Sophocles plays with several levels of consciousness, bringing them into contrast, before transcending them.

Sophocles sets a trap for all-powerful rationality with *Œdipus the King*

Everything in the play *Œdipus the King* tends to suggest that Œdipus is a monster, justly punished for transgressing taboos against incest and parricide. But seriously! Remember above all, this is a myth, then a play, which is a symbolic scenario, and not a true story! A myth, a poetic or artistic work should never be taken literally. As explained by Alan Watts, "we must be careful in using it, not to confuse image and reality, which would be equally as wrong as to climb a signpost instead of taking the road designated". Nobody seeks to reduce mythological characters to actual people or stories. The multiple figures of mythology, are half-human, half-animal beings with chronological inconsistencies, such as Hercules' exploits stealing the golden apples of the Hesperides, Prometheus stealing fire from the gods to give to men, etc.

This symbolic space of myth is precisely meant to representation irrational and unconscious stories, sometimes forbidden in real life. Moreover, it is well known that the whole point of some theatrical works is to reveal the hidden psyche in order to offer an outlet, a therapeutic catharsis. This possibility of expression through speech and action, on stage, in a mythological tale, operates as an antidote to acting out in real life. For therapy to work, the freedom offered by the symbolic space, and the word that can be freely deployed[4], is essential, as it is in psychoanalysis ordinarily.

With Œdipus' myth, Sophocles denounces the loss of symbolic and mythological dimensions that characterize the change of civilization. Shedding the light on taboo subjects is sufficient for triggering the resistances of rationality and the loss of the symbolic dimension of the story. In this way Sophocles denounces the failure of the rational approach to remain in the symbolic dimension of the ancient traditions. Making Œdipus a myth, a crisis without a future reveal what modernity did to the ancient traditions which, we shall see, have a different, much deeper reading of the myth.

If Œdipus ended up in bed with his mother after killing his father, he is also, and above all, a victim of the secret that kept him in the ignorance of the true identity of his parents since he was adopted in secret by parents suffering from infertility. If we give to self-knowledge and truth about the parentage the

---

[4] Apparently, politicians and lawmen that now punish bad language, encouraging judgmental attitude (without compassion), do not realize that by censoring verbal expression of the unconscious, a first step to integration, they increase the risk of acting out.

importance that this had to the eyes of the ancient sages, then the story takes on another meaning.

From a traditional point of view, Œdipus' real fault was not knowing himself, which is to say, he did not know his parents and origins. The incest and parricide are merely consequences. But precisely, Œdipus managed to restore the truth and that is what will save him. We can also ask: was he truly himself when he transgressed the taboo, or was he a person alienated by the secret of his origins, not yet born as a subject? Basically, all those who have not integrated their origins and so who have not emancipated themselves from their parents, are still symbolically in incest and parricide, victims of the matriarchal regime. In any case, if Œdipus had not received false information, he would have been confronted with modern wrath and could have emancipated himself from the matriarchal omnipotence in growing as a subject.

Sophocles shows how Œdipus was a victim of both the modern regime which would prohibit the discovery of its origins, and the omnipotent matriarchal who prefer the status quo. In the view of Sophocles, as long as he is alienated in the transmission of parentage (transgenerational inheritance), a person remains trapped in an incestuous and parricide symbolic position. The integration of origins, of family histories that remained in suffering and that are inherited from ancestors can free one from this infantile position, to become truly oneself. In other words, all those who do not know themselves, who have not assimilated the history of their origins, are unable to grow as subject, and like Œdipus, may remain in an incestuous and parricide symbolic state. The modern reaction involves cutting the link to the mother (and losing the link to the all being), which can only leads to the later return of the link that has been repressed. Sophocles teaches us that true emancipation is synonymous with the birth of the subject, through the restoration of the truth about the history of the origins, through the integration of unconscious transgenerational inheritance and reconnection to the source, or to the origins[5].

Because Œdipus went through the unthinkable and eventually integrates his dramatic history, a new life will be granted. So we should not stop at appearances without considering the whole story that Sophocles tells us, especially with *Œdipus at Colonus*. Why is this last work usually set aside, denigrated? Simply because in a modern perspective it is impossible to imagine a future following the transgression of taboos. The fate that awaits those who transgress taboos can only be tragic, without hope of redemption. If it were possible to break taboos like Œdipus, and yet become a hero, then where are we going?

All aficionados of pure rationality, suspicious of imagination and insensitive to the symbolism of the story fall into the trap set by Sophocles. How is it that the vast majority of specialists, even Freud, have fallen into the trap? Isn't tempting to project one's own cultural dispositions on to Œdipus, an ideal scapegoat? Filmmakers, opera creators, writers and critics, stage directors, actors, usually do not see anything else in Œdipus but the mirror

---

[5] For those who, like Oedipus, lack information on their biological families, the unknown transgenerational legacies are symbolically present in the here and now. It is the deep desire to resolve these close issues that brings us to what alienates us and which manifests itself externally to us. But the key is to reconnect with the roots, with what in mythology corresponds to Father Sky and Mother Earth, even to find a symbolic or heart family, a mythological filiation, to achieve this.

of their own modern conditioning. This general attitude shows us how difficult it is to break free from cultural conditioning that has been strengthened for almost two millennia. Besides, all those who know Œdipus simply through the reputation of having committed incest and parricide are also caught in that "superego" logic of modern mentality. By contrast, the one who does not stop at these episodes and tries to discover the true story of Œdipus becomes aware of the strength of this cultural conditioning, and thereby creates the possibly to free himself. Denouncing the consequences of our cultural conditioning and forgetfulness of ancestral wisdom is already a good reason to rediscover the true meaning of the work of Sophocles.

With *King Œdipus* Sophocles puts a stone in front of the entrance to a tunnel that leads to the traditional initiation and rite of passage through Mother Earth. It is necessary to overcome this fascination that belongs to taboos and transgression to see behind the stone and engage in the adventure that continues until Colonus. Such an approach allows Sophocles to denounce the limits of modernity that dramatizes and prevents the continuation of an ancient initiatory journey. This ban comes at the worst moment, precisely when the drama could turn into a therapeutic catharsis[6].

The quest for truth

Behind the modern interpretation of the Œdipus myth are the real messages Sophocles leaves as his legacy. These are manifold, starting with the search for truth and the question of self-

---

[6] A situation that exactly happens when what would be called an awakening in the shamanic culture, would be seen as a mental illness in the modern culture.

knowledge. This is not limited to the knowledge of one's origins (his parents and his family history), but also involves the encounter with oneself, or the arising of true self. "I looked for myself," Heraclitus explained. The development of self-knowledge proceeds, sooner or later, to integrating its origins. Among the stages of this journey, there is the integration of unconscious transgenerational inheritance and the process (or ritual) of passage from childhood to adulthood.

The Œdipus myth revolves around a quest for truth, *Aletheia* in Greek that means "not forgetting", that is to say to access this dimension that has all that was, is, and will be. Œdipus wants to know, he wants to find out the truth at all costs. And indeed he pays the price for it.

Although at the beginning of the investigation, Œdipus cannot bear to hear the truth spoken by Tiresias (that he himself is the murderer of the former king Laius and the cause of the presence of plague in Thebes), it does not turn him away from his quest to know the truth. By dint of investigating, he will discover the truth about his origins. Here he plays the heroic figure of the man who goes to the end of his quest for truth. This signs both his death and his rebirth, as Tiresias had predicted. On a plane of consciousness he loses everything, while on another level, he gains knowledge of his origins. This new knowledge is worth all the crown land, since it will allow him to be reborn and to become the benefactor and hero of Colonus. This is an illustration of the meaning given to the Greek adage, "know thyself and you shall know the gods and the universe."

Transgenerational integration

Œdipus' situation is also comparable to that of the teenager when he starts having a more objective look at his parents, idealized during childhood[7]. The discovery of the true identity of his parents has a double consequence. First, it may create disappointment, the loss of what he thought he knew, as if the ground on which he walked disappears under his feet. Faced with the consequences of this ignorance, Œdipus blames himself for trusting appearances, which is why he blinds himself at the end of King Œdipus. Although he lost the crown and he became the black sheep of all those who, still in the morning, would praise him to the skies. At the same time, Œdipus is now at another state of consciousness, buoyed by the knowledge that he now has of his origins. The life he led until then appears other, that of a victim of the secret adoption. He realizes that his own place was obviously not in his mother's bed, nor in that fatal fight with his father. If he nonetheless found himself in this position, it was because of ignorance and the lack of transmission by his entourage. This can also restore meaning to the nightmares he had while young, and to the sense of the words of the oracle, and to his victory over the Sphinx. By revisiting his history in the light of his discovery, he can finally integrate it.

As I developed in detail in my books[8], transgenerational analysis reveals the amplification over several generations of an

---

[7] One aspect that I develop in my books, where Polybius and Merope are the superficial parenting images while, in the guise of Laius and Jocasta, the appearance of the mask falls to discover a harsh reality, but also more true.

[8] *Œdipus Reborn,* (2014) and *Transgenerational Healing, New Depth Psychology* (2016), Ecodition, Geneva.

important original conflict. Coincidentally, we find in Œdipus' ancestors the same conflict between civilizations that agitated the minds of the time. Indeed, the ancestor of Œdipus, Cadmus founded the city of Thebes by generating two lineages that will fight for power. By planting the teeth of a dragon in the land, Cadmus begets Aboriginals, which therefore are children of Mother Earth, the matriarchal side. On the other side, Cadmus married a goddess, Harmony, and their children belong to the order of Olympic deities.

The conflict between these two progenies will grow over generations, unleashing a growing flood of unmourned griefs that will pass its effects down through generations. Finally, the transgenerational inheritance of these (pathological) failings will manifest through the infertile couple, Laius and Jocasta. Thus, at birth, Œdipus not only inherits the lack of integration of his parents, but also the transgenerational issues that has characterizes Thebes itself since its foundation (double lineage).

Since he has become aware of his parentage, he no longer needs to go "for real" by means of incest and parricide. He can now follow the traditional rite of passage, that of a crossing of the darkness in caves, for example, the loss of references from childhood to emerge transformed, ready to reintegrate into the community. Through the worst trials, Œdipus becomes a sacred character, whose blessing is synonymous with great benefits for those who get it. Because he was the first to grant him his hospitality, despite his terrible reputation, Œdipus will bequeath Theseus a secret that will ensure the prosperity of his kingdom. As a result of deep respect and love between these two, a symbolic filiation develops, restoring these ties of the heart that were so cruelly missing at the time of Oedipus' birth. The story that began with the plague in Thebes accordingly closes with this prosperity guarantee. But this guarantee is subject to a duty not to forget the story of Œdipus, a recommendation that fits well with the spirit of ancestor cult observed in ancient traditions.

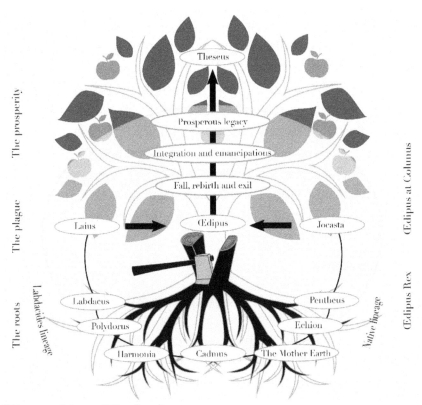

The teaching of Sophocles

The myth of Œdipus by Sophocles functions as a mirror reflecting the image that we project on it. But if one takes the trouble to follow the author, we understand that he invites us to go beyond the original conflict to find a primal unity, fertile. With the restoration of the truth and the integration of family histories,

Sophocles offers a therapeutic solution that transcends the limits of matriarchy and modernity. The lifting of secrecy about the true origin of Œdipus is a pre-condition for the advent of the subject. The matriarchal regime, represented by Jocasta and her attempt to prevent Œdipus from continuing his quest for truth, is overcome by the need to free oneself from this secret that alienates him. And when confronted with the modern regime, illustrated by Laius trying to block his path, Œdipus made it through the test. Yet these are precisely the two forces, modern and matriarchal, which block the child in a symbolically incestuous and parricidal position. Only the birth of the subject, its emancipation, can ensure empowerment from the feminine matrix without losing the relation to being. This is the problem of the modern solution that represses the link to the mother and to being. In Œdipus, the development of the subject takes the form of a renaissance, indicating a change of state of awareness, from self-ignorance to self-knowledge.

In conclusion

Since the change of civilization, a new kind of conflict has developed which it is difficult to escape. The meaning of certain traditional customs, such as ancestor cults, memory and transmission of family stories, was lost. In its efforts to overcome the matriarchal culture, the new modern civilization cuts itself off from its relation to being, the link to Mother Earth, generating all sorts of new problems. Today they are found in climate change, the pollution of rivers, procreative and intellectual sterility, the instrumentalization of natural resources (patents on seeds, GMO, etc.), where the laws written by men no longer take into account the unwritten laws of nature and life.

Our civilization has lost this consciousness of transgenerational laws. Many of us, like Œdipus, bear a lack of integration of our origins. Visionary, Sophocles was aware of the issues and consequences of this change of civilization. Based on the crisis in Athens, struck by the plague, he shares a teaching and a model to restore peace and prosperity. He shows that in the new civilization, a person can lead as a king, even if he does not know himself but knows the rhetoric (of the Sophists in the time of Sophocles). However, because he did not know himself, because he has not integrated his transgenerational unconscious legacies, that leader is carrying a conflict that manifests itself externally by the plague. But what differentiates Œdipus from other leaders is that he is determined to engage in a search for truth in order to restore the situation. He discovered that the problem was lurking inside him, in his ignorance of his parentage.

We are all concerned by this conflict of civilizations and its consequences, especially the neglect of transgenerational laws. It is time to look at the wounded being in us, to go to the source of his malaise, to restore links with the origins of life. For this, Sophocles' teaching is valuable. And the rediscovery of transgenerational phenomena in contemporary therapies has brought forth elements that were missing to understand the teaching he left us: a model of resolving a conflict between tradition and modernity for over two millennia.

If the external problems challenge and attract us, it is rather by investigating like Œdipus did that we discover ourselves, as the source of the problems that we unconsciously perpetuate projecting them on the outside. A discovery that gives us the solution, since by learning to know ourselves we develop our own potential for healing. If we have unconsciously inherited the conflict between civilizations, and its consequences (loss of self-knowledge, obliviousness to one's own family history and to one's roots from his ancestors), the story of Œdipus shows us how to transform the situation. With this hero guarantor of prosperity for his hosts, Sophocles restores most of the traditional function of shamans. But his Œdipus myth is also a myth for modern times, providing a model for what we now call a personal and spiritual development, the history of he who learned to know himself and to know the gods and universe.

Bibliography

Abraham and Torok, (1994), *The Shell and the Kernel,* University of Chicago Press.

Doods R, Eric, (2004), *The Greek and the Irrational,* University of California Press.

Dumas Didier, (1998), *La Bible et ses fantômes,* Desclée de Brouwer, Paris.

Gaillard T. Tony (2020), *Transgenerational Therapy: Healing the Inherited Burden,* Genesis Editions, Geneva.

Gaillard T. Tony (2020), *Transgenerational Healing of Oedipus at Colonus, Unveiling a universal therapeutic model,* Genesis Edition, Geneva.

Gaillard Thierry (2013), *Sophocle thérapeute. La guérison d'Œdipe à Colone,* Genesis Editions, Geneva.

Gaillard Thierry (2014), *L'intégration transgénérationnelle. Aliénations et connaissance de soi,* Genesis Editions, Geneva.

Glotz, Gustav, (1931), *Histoires Grecques,* PUF, Genève.

Jung Carl Gustav, (1966), *Ma vie, souvenirs, rêves et pensées,* Gallimard, Paris.

Jung Carl Gustav, (1990), *L'Âme et le soi, renaissance et individuation,* Albin Michel, Paris.

C. Michael Smith, (2007), *Jung and Shamanism in Dialogue,* 2nd Edition, Trafford Publishing.

Watts Alan (1989), *The Book On the Taboo Against Knowing Who You Are,* Vintage Books.

C. Michael Smith, Ph.D. (Mikkal) is a Clinical and Jungian psychologist, trained in Medical Anthropology. He is Director of *Crows Nest Centers for Shamanic Studies International,* based in the S.W. Michigan Woodlands Michigan (USA), and has formed healing-learning communities in France, Belgium, South Africa, and Iquitos, Peru. He was educated at the University of Chicago, The Chicago Theological Seminary, and the C.G. Jung Institute of Chicago. In addition to maintaining an active private practice, he is an author, keynote lecturer and workshop teacher in the field of Jungian psychology and shamanic healing. Peer reviewer for the *Journal of Anthropology of Consciousness*, he has served on numerous doctoral research committees. He is a faculty member of the French *"Cercle de Sagesse de l'Union des Traditions Ancestrales"* and was elected to *Le Collège de Chamanisme Ancestral* in 2014.

His Website http://crowsnestshamanism.com

7

Transmission and Psychoshamanism

Interview[1] of C. Michael Smith

Question 1: (Personal experience)

How much of importance was your relation to your ancestors in the path becoming a Jungian therapist and/or a shaman?

Answer: I want to say that it's pretty important as it has been to indigenous peoples and shamanic cultures all over the world. I'm a Cherokee-metis which means a mixed blood. Right now I'm sitting in the Peruvian Amazon in area where curandismo shamanism is a big element. The mestizo population here in the Amazon is also mixed bloods between Spanish descent and the different Indian tribes of the regions. As mixed-bloods we always have to build bridges with the dominant culture. But for me the Cherokee lineage that came from my mother was more about the Cherokee ethos and their stories: a lot about their encounters with the white man and the grief over the Trail of Tears, a real holocaust for the Cherokee, that sort of thing. I should mention

---

[1] Realized by Thierry Gaillard in Iquitos, Peru, (October 2015).

that "Tsalagi" is the correct spelling for Cherokee, but the later spelling has become more familiar. From my mother I received a lot of teachings around the reverence for Mother Earth, for the creativity of nature and the need to take care of nature. My mother had a lot of teachings for me around plants and how to take care of plants, and also the various healing qualities of plants, and their uplifting or grounding and relaxing qualities. My grandmother and aunt had a lot of folk remedies that were of indigenous origin.

Later, when I felt a calling toward a shamanic way of healing (I had some mystical experiences that pushed me in this direction), I ended up seeking a human teacher to help guide me. There were several places I turned to and I found an Ojibway teacher, Tom Topash, to teach me ceremonies like the Medicine Sweat, the Medicine Wheel, the Sacred Pipe, and to help me get established on the Good Red Road, the heart-path of North American tribes. But I also found of a Cherokee teacher, (Ai Gvhdi Waya), or should I say she found me? Initially she found me and invited me into a little circle with some other Jungian analysts who were learning methods of shamanic healing with her. She has met with me for more than 20 years now and she has helped me a lot. Ai Gvhdi Waya came from a family of numerous Cherokee-metis healers and even her own brother became like a brother with me in a spiritual sense so we feel like we're a part of a family.

Then later, I met Don Alberto Taxo, a Quechua Taita Iachak from Ecuador. I learned that he came from a family where his mother was a shaman and she taught him healing through conscious and reverent eating, how to create wellness through the ceremony of eating, and spirituality through eating too. Don

Alverto had a grandfather who was a Iachak who taught him much about the Iachak traditions and their simple ceremonies of eating, bathing, feeling the elements with open heart, expressing gratitude, and greeting every bringing you meet, in every time and place with an open heart: "Tu Kuy Shunguwan Kuyanimi." This is a South American Indian heart-path that approaches all of life as sacred, and has the simplest ceremonies, so simple anyone can do them. But they are profound and provide the basis of the love energy of shamanic healing and soul-fullness. When don Alverto's grandfather felt that don Alverto had sufficient preparation, they sent him to Bolivia, to Peru, and finally on to Mexico City. Each of those were apprenticeships lasting one or two years where he got to experience outside his lineage, outside his culture, learning other people's ways, and helping to keep his mind open and flexible. What interests me there is the way that you begin with root lineage, like the roots of a tree, it comes from your own ethnic origins and their shamanic principles, followed by instruction in ceremonies and healing techniques, the trunk of the tree. Once you have all of that down, you can branch out and enrich your indigenous knowledge the knowledge and experience of other cultures, to see how they do it, and extend your own shamanic knowledge.

So for me, since I did not have the richness of all that living indigenous wisdom handed down, I try to find it or create it as best I could. From my Vision Quest, when it came to looking at my future and how I am going to practice, I looked around the United States where I live and what kind of opportunities are there for me to do the work that I do. What came to me, and it came to me during Vision Quest, was that psychotherapy, becoming a psychologist maybe, would give me a place where I could put my own skills and wisdom to the service of others. This was part of my vision. And so, I went and trained at the University of Chicago, the Jung Institute of Chicago, the Chicago Theological Institute, getting credentials that my culture in the United States recognizes. So I created a kind of dialogue and synthesis of the vision of shamanic wisdom and modern depth psychology, so I had a way to relate shamanism to the culture of the white man in Western civilization. I am going to say that depth psychology, too, is a lineage, a lineage of modern Western civilization that I try to integrate into my own Cherokee ethnic roots, and shamanic calling.

Question 2: (Shamanic family)

In traditional contexts, shamanism often is passed through generation. Why? Do Westerners have to catch up something more when they want to follow that path?

Answer: When one is called by the spirit overpoweringly, tribal shamans often come through a family lineage where they've grown up watching their mother who was a healer or their father or an uncle or a grandfather who were healers, so they grew up in a world where shamanic healing was going on, and like children everywhere they were able to absorb and learn. They were at "shaman school" from day one, so, this is a great advantage obviously in learning all the ins and outs and details of shamanic practice. I would say the modern Westerner who's feeling strongly called in this direction does have to compensate for this lack and establish the equivalent kind of experiential knowledge base. They may begin with workshops and they may feel drawn to go to the jungle and work with curanderos and go to the mountain-tops and work with Paqos or go to Africa or Australia wherever they can find a traditional system still in place. But

146

ultimately I feel that in modern Western culture we have to work to develop our own system of passing it down generation after generation, through family lines, it's not the only way to pass it down but it is a very powerful way. It gives one a sense of rootedness in a natural way to learn and see it applied in life, up-close.

Another aspect of this question is the life of the shamanic parent that is kind of warts and all, or the life of the grandparent or uncle or whatever. Over-idealization is not possible. Admiration and realism remain close to each other, which is important to avoid the pitfalls of perfectionism. In the smaller indigenous village context, everybody knows everybody and the stories about the shaman are known through the community. For example they know if a local curandero or shaman is a good healer and they know if he likes women too much, or drinks too much, - but he's really good and really caring, so the child, a boy or girl, growing up in this family context has a chance to learn from that and maybe not make some of the same mistakes. A big part of initiation is learning about reality, and what goes on. Inn Western civilization, by contrast, we are more isolating and we don't have a tight community. And so people don't know about their immediate ancestors and theirs secrets. And what we don't know about our parents and grandparents, and aunts and uncles, give us troubling issues in the family that can be repeated over and over again. So there's more work for us to do and more discoveries to be made, and doing our own inner wounded healer work in order for us Western-style shamans must do before we can catch up with our indigenous counterparts.

Question 3: (About today)

In your book, **Jung and Shamanism in Dialogue²,** *you claim that shamanism always adapted to changing circumstances. Can you say more about that statement?*

Answer: Yes, in traditional societies, shamanic cultures are in process and change all the time. At more distant times, they were nomadic, moving around the jungle, moving around the plains, moving around the mountains. Not exhausting the supplies of an area, but living in some relative balance with the area and the food source. They tended to be good eco-psychologists.

So, in essence they had to change all the time, and the change of locality would change the mythology, you know, the kind of map of reality people lived by. And so if things changed, that had to be reflected in the guiding mythology. The people who do that sort of re-visioning would be the vision seekers, the shamans, and elders of the community, and they would have to take the changes that come about, both in the geography and in the climate, and consider how this must be reflected in the mythology so that the people have a map that mirrors their currently reality and which gives them a sense of the possibilities and principles of wellness in it.

So one function then is the shaman as the creative re-mythologizer who is constantly evolving the theoretical and imaginal background of the people so they have a set of principles and guiding images to live by that resonates and articulates with the environment in which they actually live.

---

² C. Michael Smith, (2007), *Jung and Shamanism in Dialogue,* 2nd Edition, Trafford Publishing.

C. Michael Smith

But other things beyond change in climate or geography could happen, there could be warfare, there could be tragedy and loss, again bringing forth the need to re-vision the mythology and add to the stories. As is happening all over the place today, theres a collision between Western civilization and colonialism with indigenous, heart-open and earth-honoring ways of life. So you can find shamans in the Amazon, indigenous and Mestizo shamans here in the Peruvian Amazon who are using cell phones and know how to get internet access and this sort of thing. Some of them I've seen baptize these new technologies, and smoke them down with *mapacho* and purify them and give them the dignity of a name and then use them because it's infiltrating the world everywhere and that fact is probably not going to stop or to be changed. But how to put the it into integrity with the mythology people live by, which supports a heart open and Earth honoring way of life? It is a big challenge. Because things are always changing, we previously had shamans who kept their minds and their belief systems open and fluid enough so that they could help guide the community in ways that resonated with the reality they were currently living in.

I was saying earlier that I'm a Cherokee-metis. There's another way, let's say I'm a shamanic healer, I'm on that path, but I also have to do it in terms of the modern culture United States, Europe, South Africa, other places where I'm working and teaching. It's important to be shamanic and yet speak the language of your own culture, to create a bridge between the shamanic world and the modern world of science, biology, in my case depth psychology. This is something that people believe in and they go to psychotherapist for with their problems. This is a "place" I work in, so I have a "place," a validated "social location" to practice from, and that is my psychotherapy and analytic practice. But at the same time, I have the task of trying to promote shamanism by dialoguing, integrating, synthesizing shamanism with psychotherapy. This is so that when people do have shamanic experiences, when they do go to the jungle or the high Andes or to central Africa or wherever they go for indigenous teachings and experiences they can bring that back into their own culture, so that they can really integrate it actually implement it, have a way of passing it onto others that the culture will accept.

In the end, this dialogue between psychology and shamanism leads to an enrichment both ways. It's helping to enrich traditional shamanism and give new tools of understanding in indigenous context, in Mestizo context. I see how the concepts of the unconscious and of transference are enriching shamanic knowledge in the Amazon, as they work with Western seekers of healing and shamanic knowledge. The shaman's, especially the mestizo curanderos, are learning the language of Western healing systems to better help their Western clients, and giving them knew perspectives on their own work. At the same time the modern Western shamanic healer as deepening and extending the power of psychotherapy to actually help people heal with trauma. Ancient wisdom is coming into psychotherapy and bringing it real ontological power beyond mere technique. The life and work of C.G. Jung, as I have carefully documented, is highly aligned with this development, which is what it has been such a bridge making conceptual foundation for me. It offers an equivalent of a Western mythology that makes room for shamanic wisdom.

Question 4: (Possible adaptation of shamanism)

You are providing a psycho-shamanic training. Is that a form of modern shamanism? Does it mean that you take distance from root shamanism?

Answer: *Psychoshamanism* is a word that I am using to describe the way I have bridged modern western healing method that comes through psychotherapy, particularly Jungian and depth psychology, with the more ancient and indigenous shamanism that I have studied and developed into my own craft, as a healer. In it I have moved beyond scholarly dialogue between Jungian psychology and shamanism, into a synthesis. In practice, over nearly four decades, it has become fairly seamless and one, for me. Yet I recognize I do have to bridge things for my Western clients.

The fact is that most of my clients and students are from Western civilization, Europe, South Africa, United States. So part of their mythology is science, medicine, depth psychology, clinical psychology, this sort of thing. In that regard, I am a bridge maker, as mestizo shamans have always been (mixed bloods). We are not in one culture to the exclusion of another, we still have to bridge cultures, so both sides, both points of view, so to speak, know what's going on in the other.

Psychoshamanism, we could say, is about the synthesis of two different kinds of mythologies, with respect to living well and caring for the planet and healing with profound power. All this together is psychoshamanic healing. From another point of view, any healing that does not include the power of love, of an open-heart and earth-honoring way of life, of community, of ancestry, is out of congruence with reality. Psychoshamanism is about genuine healing, about accepting the universal aspects of reality, accepting what is, but keeping open and centered enough to be directive and free at the same time.

Does it take me a distance from traditional root shamanism? Yes it does, but as we have been saying, everything is in flux and changing and evolving. It has never been the business of Shamanism to just repeat the past. Shamanism in its visionary aspect must always creatively reinterpret the past along ways that illuminate the present and help us adapt towards what's coming in the future, and shape it in heart-open and earth-honoring ways. So I think I am doing what shamanic healers and elders have always done, I'm creatively re-visioning the mythologies of my culture as a modern person, and at the same time contributing to the indigenous shamanic world and practices, bringing some tools that help us understand that world and make use of it in a way that will be rooted and solid in our own cultures.

There is no point in going to the Peruvian Amazon and doing Ayahuasca or going to the High Andes and doing San Pedro, if you can't make use of that experience in the world that you live in. So that's what Psychoshamanism in part is about and what the *Jung and Shamanism in Dialogue* is about. In the Amazon, my events are retreats and workshops called *JUNG AND SHAMANISM IN SYNTHESIS.*

Question 5: (Healing the soul or suppressing symptoms)

Sciences and epigenetic have proven that trauma are passed on descendant. Shamanism already has tools to heal these issues. Do you think medical treatment will do a better job? Why?

Answer: Recently in medical science there's discoveries that epigenes themselves can be passed on and the way they turn on or off a gene sequence, or segment, this also can be passed on. But epigenes are what ride on top of the chromatin and actually block the expression of some portion of a segment of DNA that might actually promote healthy expression in your life. But when that's shut down it predisposes to you some type of dysfunction.

And a lot of what's been found through epigenetic research is that changes in attitudes, changes in consciousness can create changes at the psychological level and at the biological level.

Maybe it's somewhat in line what's known in the field of clinical hypnosis as a placebo effect, the power of consciousness to suggestively or intentionally actually act upon the genes and change what is happening there, being expressed there.

So the question is, do I think medical treatment will do a better job, if so why? And I really don't know the answer to that, but I don't think the solution is simply going into the genetic or epigenetic level and making changes mechanically for the person, while bypassing the consciousness of the being who has that body, who has that DNA and those epigenes.

Something is lost if we don't' know how to change ourselves, if we don't know how to heal ourselves, shift our consciousness in a way that makes our bodies healthier, even at the level of epigenetics, even at the level of DNA.

So I think the old Newtonian/Cartesian framework that's still alive in medicine thinks that mechanically extracting something is the cure but I think from my own shamanic perspective you cannot bypass the person who has this trauma. They must become conscious. They must become an active participant in their healing.

Question 6: (Transmission)

Transmission through generation is minimalized in Westerner culture, but used to be very important in traditional culture. How much do you think transgenerational integration can help people to be rooted and eventually feel more balanced in life?

Answer: By transmission I'll say that's the passing on of knowledge or principals or techniques that are useful and handing them down to subsequent generations. Every culture does this in one form or another.

In modern Western culture, so much transmission is impersonal and handed down academically, or through science, through journals through reports and of course we have a lot on the internet and so on. But the kind of transmission that is transmitting data or information can be quite impersonal.

In indigenous cultures, the kind of transmission that happens is much more alive and holistic, and it comes through storytelling and the sharing of personal events that happen to the people telling the stories. Even the codes of ethics acted out in puberty rites are like a psychodrama displaying in 3-D form before the young men and women and how they ought to live and what they ought not to do. It is communicated through story, and it's through storytelling in ritual context, -even personal disclosures, in indigenous cultures that so much wisdom is handed down.

It's not just the verbal, but also the non-verbal aspects of something that's handed down that are important. For example, in Ecuador the concept of becoming an Ancestor, a good Ancestor, is one of the great aims of life. You can't learn to do it from a book, and it's not about leaving a good book behind, it's also not to leave a story behind in the usual sense of that, but it's to leave so much love behind and kindness and respect that it's enfolded in the hearts of your children and your grandchildren. And one generation after another is passing this loving energy on.

This is a way of being in the world that is heart open, that's earth honoring and reverent. So yes we need this, and this is sadly lacking so much in modern Western civilization. I think we need it so we can live in a more balanced way with each other and with mother earth. I will die happy in the knowledge that my children, my students, have enfolded in their heart the best love that I can give them. Because if they have that, I know that they're going pass it on.

9 782940 540402